Joy to You and Me (At Work!)

Amy Thornton

Joy to You and Me (At Work!)

©2018, Amy Thornton
Wise Words Publishing, a subsidiary of:
Tell-Tale Publishing Group, LLC
Swartz Creek, MI 48437

All rights reserved. No portion of this publication may be reproduced, stored in an electronic system, or transmitted in any form or by any means, electronic, mechanical, photocopy, recording, or otherwise, without the prior permission of Amy Thornton. Brief quotations may be used in literary reviews.

Printed in the United States of America

This book is dedicated to the family members, friends, colleagues, teachers, and others who supported and encouraged me to reach my dream of becoming an author. If you've given me advice, bought one of my books, said a friendly word, pushed me to become a better writer, attended a book signing, or simply endured my craziness as I've written this book, this dedication is for you. Thank you from the depths of my heart.

"Everybody's Working for the Weekend," *Loverboy, 1981*

"I don't want to work, I want to bang on the drum all day," *Todd Rundgren, 1982*

"I'm on vacation, every single day, 'cause I love my occupation," *Dirty Heads, 2017*

Table of Contents

Introduction 1
Part One 9
Chapter One 11
Chapter Two 21
Chapter Three 27
Chapter Four 45
Part Two 69
Chapter Five 71
Chapter Six 75
Chapter Seven 83
Chapter Eight 95
Chapter Nine 109
Chapter Ten 117
Part Three 125
Chapter Eleven 127
Chapter Twelve 133
Chapter Thirteen 141
Chapter Fourteen 157
Part Four 161
Chapter Fifteen 163
Chapter Sixteen 175
Book Discussion Questions 181
About the Author 183

Introduction

(Or, Why Should We Care About Bringing Joy into the Workplace?)

An article in Forbes Magazine from January 20, 2014 entitled "8 Common Causes of Workplace Demotivation," states that most people can't say they truly love their jobs.[1] Studies show that 48% of employees worldwide don't even *like* their jobs, more than 80% of US workers feel stressed at the office, and only 30% feel "engaged and inspired" by their careers. What should really bother leaders and business owners is that 18% are actively *disengaged* – they're present at work but they hate every minute of it.[2]

To examine some more depressing reality, let's do a little math. We've all heard the saying that people spend more waking hours at work than they do with their family. According to a survey conducted by Gallup in the summer of 2014, the new average for most full-time workers has risen from 40 to 46-47 hours per week.[3] That basically means workers are only getting one true day off instead of the normal two days.

But wait, what if you're one of the lucky ones whose full time job is actually 40 hours a week? You still spend about 50 waking hours per week at work (factoring in the average half-hour commute and one hour lunch break) vs. about 62 waking hours at home. That's just a little less than half our waking lives spent at work.

So, to put it simply: a lot of us are unhappy campers in our workplaces and we're spending a big ol' chunk of our lives there.

To prevent everyone from wanting to leap off the top of the nearest cliff or tallest building, let's examine how we can turn this picture around – and do it quickly.

The good news is that two of the biggest causes for a lack of workplace motivation are actually *within our control* - unpleasant co-workers and boredom. But wait, we can't really change other people, right? True, but we *can* make certain we're not one of those unpleasant co-workers. And we can take easy steps to genuinely brighten everyone's workday, even the Mr. and Mrs. Grumpy Butts of the world. As an added bonus, these steps not only reduce boredom, they actually kick it to the curb!

Being positive and joyful isn't just a fluffy-cutesy-nice thing to do each day - it actually increases productivity and is vitally important for any company or organization.

Gallup research has shown for years that strong work friendships boost employee satisfaction by 50%, and people with a best friend at work are seven times more likely to engage fully in their tasks.[4] We don't *have* to have our "best buds in the world" at work, but we do need to be able to relax around our colleagues and enjoy their company.

Forbes states in a hopeful March 6, 2017 article, "Millennials, Here's Why You're Dissatisfied at Work," that studies show a clear link between strong employee ties and a business's overall output.[5] As team bonds strengthen, productivity and sales increase—31 to 37% on average, according to the Harvard Business Review.[6] This magazine also stated that research proves when people work with a positive mind-set, performance on nearly every level—productivity, creativity, and engagement—improves.

Joy to You and Me (At Work!)

Most people think happiness is some destination we *arrive at* vs. *create* within ourselves. But Folks, it's up to us to change to a more joyful mindset, and to spread that joy to others, whether we're at an entry level, middle, or top position in a company or organization. We can make a huge difference by doing quick, simple things each day to improve our workplace.

Imagine spending those hours we talked about earlier being happy and productive, making a difference in the lives of those around us, and showing the world just what an asset we are! There are surprisingly easy ways to do this, but they're not taught in most schools. It all starts with a simple focus on bringing joy to the workplace.

I've been bringing joy to my workplaces for over 25 years. I have an innate enthusiasm and extensive training on how to spread it to others for the improvement of entire companies. Right out of college, I consistently broke sales records as the advertising director for a Central Indiana newspaper due to my joyful interactions with customers. As a customer service representative for a biotechnology company in Indianapolis, I frequently won Employee of the Month thanks to going above and beyond for my co-workers and customers.

My formal training on bringing joy to others began when I took the Dale Carnegie Human Relations Course in 1995. I was instantly hooked on the course's principles. I moved on to become a graduate assistant for the class in 1996 and an instructor from 1998 - 2008. I continued to "practice what I preached" to bring enthusiasm to my Town of Field's Corner, Indiana teammates and the people we served, which was proven in 2009 when I received the Town's Stake in the Ground award. The town council gives this award--which is literally a wooden stake--to a town employee who makes a positive difference for the community and the municipality in general.

I've done well in my various positions through the years, but almost all of my current or former bosses will tell you that I was hired for each of them because of my enthusiasm, and I succeeded in those positions due to that trait. Yes, I've done my jobs well, but I'm not a genius. And you don't have to be a genius to make a difference.

This book will give you quick, easy tips you can use starting *today* in whatever position you're in, whether you work in a factory, big box store, corporation, non-profit, or anything else. I'll share real-life stories to show how you can be a more joyful person. I'll talk about how to spread that joy to your co-workers, customers, and those you network with. These stories come from my life and others and take place in non-profits, small companies, and global enterprises.

The book will also explain *why* it is so crucial for us to work on this joy almost every day.

Before we move on to the fun, I thought it would be good to address some potential real-life "what the heck?" questions you may have.

Frequently Asked Questions

1. I'm just a peon, how can I make a difference in my company?

Good question. I've been a peon at work lots of times! I was just an entry level customer service representative with the previously mentioned biotechnology company, but that didn't stop me from doing little things here and there to brighten peoples' days. And when I say little, I mean it--maybe five minutes here and there, which added up to a lot and helped me win Employee of the Month many times. Stick with me, and you won't be a peon for long.

2. *Yeah, but I'm just a kid in high school . . . or about to retire . . . or a part-time worker. Why should I bother with this stuff?*

So maybe you're a teenager in your first part-time job. You want to progress at least a little in this company and leave in the future on a good note, right? Every job is a stepping-stone toward your professional goals. You'll take your experiences and skills and build on them as you move along in life. So why not "wow" your fellow employees, bosses, and customers by doing things better than other young 'uns? You might even get some raises quicker than you ever imagined.

Or maybe you're about to retire and have done things the same way your whole life, and you've done pretty darn well. Good for you! But why not teach those you'll be leaving behind how to be *even better* at their jobs? Why not leave a legacy for everyone to remember in the years to come? Can't you just hear the conversation now around the water cooler? "Wow, that Joe Schmoe was great before, but he really knocked our socks off right before he left. I sure miss him."

Part-time workers? Trust me, if you start using even half the tips in this book, you'll be seen as an incredibly valuable team member and you won't be part-time for long, unless you want to stay that way.

3. *But I work from home. How can I do anything to spread joy to my workplace? I'm not there most of the time.*

I've worked from home a time or two as well. In fact, I work from home for my day job right now. But I still see co-workers and customers at various events or for team meetings. And most of the time if you're working from home, you're still interacting with these people virtually or on the phone. Many ideas in this book can be done without ever seeing someone in person. You'll become so awesome that people will actually look forward to your next email, phone call, Face Time session, etc.

4. *My job is okay and it pays the bills. Why should I bother to do this stuff?*

If you really think about it, wouldn't it make more sense to spend half of your waking hours going beyond "okay"? This is your life, people. You only get one. Even if you believe in reincarnation, isn't it better to have a bunch of kick-butt, "what a ride that was!" lives instead of "yeah, that was okay" ones?

If you're still not buying this, prove me wrong. Do a couple of things differently thanks to this book, see how they elevate your workplace from "okay" to "awesome," and do a comparison of the "before" and "after." I think you'll like the latter and be glad you took a little time to make a difference.

5. *I don't have the time or the money for this stuff. I can barely do my regular duties! How do you expect me to do the things you suggest in this book?*

I hear you. I've been there. Some of my closest family members and friends are probably thinking the same thing.

Trust me when I tell you that most of the tips shared in this book take barely any time and effort and are free or low cost. You want to do things that *increase* the productivity of your company, not take away from it. You want to be happier in your workplace and make others happier, not increase stress levels. Read a little bit of this book each week, do a couple of steps here and there, and you'll find that they actually make it easier to do your tasks!

And when I say a couple of steps, I mean it. You don't have to do every single thing in this book to start turning things around in your workplace. I talk more about this in the final Q and A, which just happens to be next.

6. I'm not outgoing like you. How can I spread joy?

I love my introverted family members, friends, and co-workers. I actually have some introverted tendencies myself. I recognize that not everyone is energetic and enthusiastic like me. That's okay. The world needs all types of people. Joyful people can be bouncy, funny, rather loud, and outgoing. But they can also be calm, wise, quiet, and introspective - or a mix of all these traits.

When I taught the Dale Carnegie course on people skills, we talked about the different ways we can be enthusiastic. There is such a thing as quiet enthusiasm, and it is downright beautiful.

You don't have to do every single thing in this book in order to bring joy to your workplace. Even the more subdued, quiet, "under the radar" tactics can bring about noticeable changes for all.

Hopefully I've helped you understand just what a big deal this joy stuff is and that it's easy to spread it around and elevate our workplaces to incredible new levels.

So let's get started on this journey, shall we?

Part One

How to Be a More Joyful Person

Amy Thornton

"Act enthusiastic and you will be enthusiastic," *Dale Carnegie, Author of How to Win Friends and Influence People*

Chapter One

It All Starts with You

You picked out this book and started reading it for a reason. Maybe you think you are part of the depressing statistics from the introduction and you are literally dragging yourself out of bed every morning to go into work. Perhaps things are OK at your job but you yearn for more enjoyment or a promotion. Or maybe you just want to shake things up a little and make people smile more often. There's only one place to start, and that's with you.

If you're not a joyful person, there is no way you can make others joyful. I'm not saying we're going to discover the secret to happiness here, but we sure can't bring joy to our careers if we're Negative Nellies (or Nelsons!). Enthusiasm is downright contagious. Unfortunately, so is a negative attitude. You have to work on yourself first in order to change things at your job. And you have to do this with sincerity. If you truly are not a happy person, people will see right through you. Remember, I'm not talking about being all crazy, goofy, and bouncing off the walls. I'm talking about how you can be joyful in a way that suits you.

Let's step back and talk about why a person with the right attitude is more successful at work so you remember the importance of working on your own mindset first.

Amy Thornton

Happy Workers Really Do Get Stuff Done

According to entrepreneur.com, 80 percent of our success is based on our EQ, and 20 percent is based on our IQ.[7] Most people know what IQ is, but not everyone has heard of EQ. EQ is your emotional quotient. Influential Harvard theorist Howard Gardner states that, "EQ is the level of your ability to understand other people, what motivates them and how to work cooperatively with them."[8]

Skills can be taught, but WE have to work on and improve our attitudes. No one else can do it for us. When you have a positive attitude, you're more open and motivated to learning new things. You're also more adaptable.

In my experience, throwing enthusiasm into the tasks I dread at work is especially helpful. I am more of a writer than a mathematician. In fact, anyone who knows me is probably snickering right now. I'm the one who passed Algebra II in high school just because the teacher felt sorry for me. But as our middle and high school teachers told us, most professions involve at least a little math.

One of my duties as office coordinator for our county's soil and water conservation district involved using QuickBooks for accounts payable and receivable. I implemented and used QuickBooks for a small company I worked for in the late 90s, so I wasn't concerned with using it in 2016. But oh, how things had changed! However, I was determined to master it and not let it defeat me.

So whenever it was time to do the "fun" stuff like reconciliation reports, I always made certain I was in the right frame of mind. I put in my ear bud to listen to some kick ass music, made my favorite cup of tea, and had a good snack nearby in case my energy dropped. I promised myself a reward once I was finished, like a walk home for lunch or at least a good stretch. And I would literally do a little happy dance whenever I had correctly completed certain reports for my boss. I began to see mastering QuickBooks as a challenge rather than a burden, and when I left the position I was pleased with my progress.

In fact, I was hired at the soil and water conservation district because of my good attitude. I didn't find this out until I had my first review. When my boss casually told me that he brought me on staff because of my personality, tears sprang to my eyes. He was definitely taken aback. Little did he know that the boss I had before him said that my personality grated on his nerves! This is a great example of how, in rare instances, some of your co-workers won't like a positive personality. But we'll discuss that more in a later chapter.

I could've complained about QuickBooks, but that wouldn't have gotten anything done. By being positive, my coworker Clarissa gladly helped me through the tough times with the program because I wasn't overly upset about my troubles with it.

Being joyful also helps conserve your energy level, while negativity often drains it. Let's face it - we never saw Eeyore getting a lot done in the Winnie the Pooh stories by A.A. Milne did we? Although I sure thought he was lovable at times! But I digress. Being positive creates momentum that can help you accomplish more than you ever imagined. And it will make others want to be around you and to help you as Clarissa often did for me. Which brings me to the next part.

Be An Asset, Not An Ass

I think everyone can agree with the previous sentence, don't you? But how often do we let negative situations bring out the worst in us, especially in our workplaces? It's easy to do. Anger can take over before we know it.

One of my favorite tips for the workplace is to always give yourself at least 24 hours before responding to someone who is upsetting you, if possible. This has saved me from acting like an ass countless times! It's like a "time out" for grown-ups. These are the situations that can make or break us. Why wait those 24 hours? That time can help you:

1. See things from the other person's point of view. This is a classic Dale Carnegie principle. Most instructors would agree that it is one of the most important concepts for improving our relationships with others. Nine times out of ten, a person is not upset with you, but rather the situation. As I write this, it's just after Christmas. This time of year used to be a difficult one in our household because my husband John managed a Mailboxes Etc., now called the UPS Store. Packages were sometimes delayed for one reason or another and many times it wasn't his store's fault. But John would always listen and try to understand the other person's situation. There may have been some venting once he got home, but he kept his cool when customers were upset. Which leads me to the next reason for a time out.

2. Find a safe person to vent to. My best friend has helped me keep my cool many times throughout different positions. Even though she lives far away, a quick email or text often helps me calm down even if she can't respond right

away. If you don't have an understanding friend or coworker who can help you get through those rough times, find one! You just might be able to help each other.

3. Create a positive response. We've all heard the saying that there are always two sides to every story. Even if you are certain the other person is wrong and shouldn't be getting upset with you, there is some reason for their reaction. Remember my nemesis QuickBooks earlier? I once received a nasty email from one of my bosses about turning in a QuickBooks report too early to the State of Indiana. When I looked up the guidelines for this report, I found out that I was correct with my timing. It would've been easy to just explode, especially knowing that I was right. But instead I took a break from the situation before responding to her. I apologized for not speaking with her first before submitting the report and let her know how much I appreciated her concern for doing things the right way. When we both had a calm moment a couple of days later, I showed her the guidelines. Things weren't all hearts and flowers after that, but our relationship was saved.

Remember, it's easy to be positive when everything is going right at work. We always show our true character with how we behave when things get tough. That's our opportunity to prove that we're assets to our company, not asses. By still holding on to just a smidge of positivity even during those low points, we can be more productive because we're not stuck in the negative world being whiny and getting nothing done.

Amy Thornton

Look Forward to Your Work Day Instead of Dragging Yourself into It

I can say with 100 percent honesty that I looked forward to almost every workday during my time with the Town of Field's Corner, even after weekends, vacations, and holidays. This attitude helped me arrive early nearly every day, and I'm not even a morning person! And by starting off my day with this attitude most of the time, I dove into my tasks and accomplished things quickly. By starting the day off right, it typically sets the tone for success. We'll talk about how to begin your day well in the next chapter.

The Little Things Won't Knock You Down

Have you heard about the emerald ash borer beetle? This little guy has been destroying millions of ash trees in the United States since 2002. It has cost municipalities, property owners, nursery operators, and forest industries hundreds of millions of dollars. Chances are your own community has been affected.

When I first heard about this beetle, I imagined some horrible, huge monstrosity that was as big as my thumb - or maybe both thumbs combined. Surely something causing this much damage must be gigantic, right? Nope. It's smaller than a penny. In fact it's the larva that causes the major problems with these poor trees. And of course they're miniscule compared to the adults!

Like the ash borer and the ash trees, it's usually the little things that often bring us down in life, especially in our work life. That delayed shipment, a caustic remark from a customer, or the "not quite as perfect as we hoped," presentation can bother us for hours. Or days. But when we look back on these issues, if we even remember them, we realize they weren't such a big deal. Being joyful in our jobs can help us combat these little problems, give us perspective on them, and prevent them from growing into big problems. It can greatly reduce our stress levels so we won't be taken down like the ash trees. We can shake off those minuscule, often unimportant situations and focus on the more urgent ones.

More Moola, Baby!

If you need one final reason for why you should be a more positive person at work, it's this - More. Money. People think that money brings happiness, but often the opposite is true. In fact, a June, 2015 article in Forbes points to studies that reveal that happier people actually earn more money.[9] Researchers found that high levels of cynicism are associated with lower incomes all over the world.[10] According to one study, after nine years, negative employees earned an average of $300 less per month than their more positive counterparts.

Let's take one profession – sales, something that most of us would agree is a tough job. Optimistic salespeople close more deals. Remember that whole enthusiasm is contagious thing? A sales person's mindset and view often rub off on his or her customers. Think about the last major purchase you made. Was the sales person grumpy or pleasant? Why did you buy this product from that individual versus another? If the products were about the same price, chances are it was his or her attitude that tipped the scales.

Amy Thornton

I recently had my Mini Cooper serviced. I adore my blue and white 2007 Mini Cooper S - in fact I firmly believe the S stands for "spectacular" and no one is going to tell me any different. Unfortunately my lovely MC, as I call it, needed some repairs last summer. My husband and I shopped around for the best place and believe it or not, we chose Reggie's, which was a little more expensive. Why? Each and every person we spoke with was positive. We could hear it in everyone's voice. The employees at Reggie's went above and beyond from the very start. They gave me cookies from my favorite local bakery when I picked up the vehicle. They even delivered bad news to me in a cheerful manner.

That, my friend, is good salesmanship and just one of many examples about how a great attitude can help you earn more money.

With all these awesome reasons for why it's important for you to be joyful at your workplace, I'm sure you're just chomping at the bit to learn how you can make that happen. I can't wait to tell you!

Joy to You and Me (At Work!)

"Working happier accomplishes much more than working harder."
Sarah Ban Breathnach, author of Simple Abundance

Chapter Two

Bringing Joy to YOU

I've been a cheerful person for as long as I can remember, even back in the dinosaur ages, a.k.a., my high school years. I was a quiet cheerful person back then, as I was a bit of a nerd and nervous about talking to people. OK, I was a certified nerd. I had acne, braces, glasses, and even a back brace for scoliosis. Yes, I had it all. Thankfully those souvenirs of adolescence went away as I approached age 18 and moved on to college at Indiana University in Bloomington.

College can be a wonderful confidence booster for many former nerds. I drove the van for disabled students and faculty as a part-time job and enjoyed getting to know my passengers. I remember one of them nicknamed me "Sunshine." I found "my people" during my sophomore year when I joined Alpha Phi Omega, a co-ed service fraternity. I loved doing volunteer work for different organizations in and around Bloomington. Our chapter was quite busy with various service projects the entire school year.

During the summer between my sophomore and junior year, I saw a rubber duck race in South Bend, Indiana that benefited the March of Dimes. I instantly fell in love with the event. This organization means a lot to me and to my family, as it helped us with my sister who had birth defects and eventually died from them before I was even born. I was determined to re-create this event with the help of my service fraternity at IU the following spring.

But how would I convince my friends to take on yet another project? I knew once we started that everyone would have fun and we could raise some decent funds for the Columbus, Indiana March of Dimes, which was the closest branch to campus. I needed to do something to grab everyone's attention, pique their interest, and get them excited.

In October, my friend Cathi made a duck costume and wore it for a Halloween party. That gave me an idea. I asked Cathi for a favor and our chapter president for five minutes of time during the next meeting.

That Sunday evening, I donned orange tights, big floppy webbed feet, a beautifully sewn yellow blob of felt with arm and leg holes, and a duck nose. When the president introduced me, I rushed up from the back and leapt in front of the chalkboard.

"Hi, guys," I exclaimed. "I'm here to tell you about a really cool event that you're going to love and we're going to put on next May."

Within 10 minutes I had eight friends sign up for the committee and we set our first meeting. And despite some challenges during the spring, such as a lack of rain that forced us to push the ducks down the Jordan River running through campus, we had a blast. The community loved it and we raised over $1000. Not bad for a first annual event put on by a small group of college kids back in 1991.

And wouldn't you know it? I won the Most Enthusiastic Award for my chapter that year and the following year as well.

It didn't hit me until after graduation that I was onto something big, something that Mr. Carnegie called the little known secret to success - enthusiasm.

Joy to You and Me (At Work!)

Thanks to a brief stint in Amway in 1995, I read his classic book, *How to Win Friends and Influence People.* This set me on a path that changed my life. I practically devoured the book and read it three times. By the third time, I knew I had to learn more, and I saw that there was a course based on this and other Dale Carnegie books. With the help of my employer, I took the Dale Carnegie human relations course that same year.

I'll never forget something one of my instructors said on the first night. She stated that we would learn how to work smarter, not harder. Even just barely starting in my working life, I saw how easily people could get burnt out in their jobs. I didn't want to be one of those people who sacrificed their family and friends for work. But I wanted to do my best in whatever job I held. I went on to become a graduate assistant for the course starting in 1996 and a full-fledged instructor in 1998, teaching for a total of 10 years.

I was already cheerful and enthusiastic at work, but this class helped me start to do more. I tried to listen to others better and talk less. I started to do some creative things to celebrate my coworkers' birthdays and other special occasions. I got to know my customers on the phone and began to ask them questions about how their lives were going. I made friends all around the country, and I'm still friends with some of them to this day.

I won Employee of the Month the following year. And won it again a couple months later. I began to see work as fun and to realize that another statement from Mr. Carnegie was true. Most of the time people don't love their jobs right from the start. Instead, they put a great deal of effort into finding numerous ways to *help them love it eventually.* Being a customer service representative and often taking complaints on the phone every hour was not what I dreamt of doing what I was a little girl. My ultimate goal was to become an author. But I decided not to just "make the best of things," but to go above and beyond for my customers, coworkers, and bosses, and to be enthusiastic every step of the way. And soon, I could say I honestly loved my job, and I have loved almost every one of them since.

As I said in the introduction, I know or believe it was my attitude that helped me get hired for nearly all of my positions. I was hired to work as the Grant Coordinator for the Town of Field's Corner, Indiana in early 2007, beating out dozens of candidates. And this was after having accidentally taken the town manager's parking space in front of the town hall a couple of years previously – right before he pulled up to park in it! But he got to know me through my community activities and it quickly became a joke between us.

I have been blessed with a naturally cheerful personality. For years, my mission in life has been to bring joy to others. But I realize not everyone is like me, especially when it comes to being positive at work. I'm probably at the extreme end of the spectrum!

It's time to stop telling my story and instead talk about the numerous ways YOU can become a more joyful person and be an example for others in your workplace. This is where we get to the good stuff, Folks!

Joy to You and Me (At Work!)

"The only way to do great work is to love what you do."
Steve Jobs

Chapter Three

Easy Joyful Ideas

No matter what kind of personality you have, you can become a more joyful person. How much more is up to you. Maybe you just need a little boost. You're fairly chipper, but would like to get some new tips. Perhaps you know you need some improvement and just want some guidance here and there.

Or, maybe your boss has flat out told you that you need to work on your attitude to improve your career - or else! I hope that's not your situation, but no matter where you are currently, this chapter will give you plenty of great ideas. You might want to keep a notebook or your mobile device handy to take some notes on your favorite ideas along the way throughout this and future chapters. The first part involves becoming the healthiest person you can possibly be. Please keep in mind I am not a doctor of any sort, so if you are dealing with a disease, major injury, or chronic illness, I encourage you to continue to work with a medical professional. And if you are dealing with a drug, alcohol, or tobacco addiction, please find the best local resources to get you on the path to better health.

So you've got to feel good in order to "do good" right? We definitely can't be joyful if our bodies aren't emotionally, mentally, physically, and spiritually healthy. Even I can't be my enthusiastic little self when I'm tired, sad, injured, or sick. So here are some things we all have to do:

Exercise

This word either makes people shudder or nod in agreement. We all know it's one of the basics for good health. Unfortunately most people's thoughts lean toward early mornings at the gym, running marathons, lifting weights, or other monumentally challenging ways to move their bodies. But that often sets us up for failure if we've never done those things before. Instead, if you're not currently exercising, start with something small.

I actually didn't exercise regularly until 2007 when I started my job with the Town of Field's Corner. Town Hall was only 10 blocks away, and I figured it would be fun to walk to and from work and also a way to save on gas. My almost daily walks were not only good for my physical health, but my mental state as well. I began to do walking meditations. It was an awesome way for me to relieve stress and tension.

I don't think walking gets the credit it deserves for exercise. But it can be extremely beneficial. My nephew Ben, for example, lost 60 pounds by just watching what he ate and walking every day. No wonder NBC News reported in September of 2017 that walking is the most underrated form of exercise![11]

Walking was definitely my "something small" and it's a great first step for many people who have never really exercised before. It's a lower impact activity and is a good option for people who are overweight or are dealing with knee, ankle, and back problems. In fact, Ben has had issues with his back since he was a teenager.

It's also simple to do nearly every day. I work from home now, so I walk my dogs early in the morning before my workday begins and sometimes on my lunch hours. I make certain to take a longer walk on the weekends. I'm currently training to walk a half marathon in the spring.

Many companies are making it easier for people to walk and do other exercises. The Town of Field's Corner created a walking path in the basement of Town Hall that is 1/15 of a mile. And thanks to a grant that provided new exercise equipment to all of our fire stations to help our public safety folks stay healthy, we were able to put some of their old equipment in that same basement for a workout room.

According to a Time Magazine article from May 2009, nearly 6 in 10 big companies are offering some sort of wellness program.[12] One of the companies that does this particularly well is Salesforce, who recently received naming rights to the largest building in Indianapolis thanks to its high occupancy and is one of my organization's partners. To put it simply, Salesforce provides technology for customer relationship management. They have over 150,000 customers and are currently located in eight cities in the United States. Salesforce has been recognized by Fortune Magazine, Indeed.com, and many other groups as one of the top places to work in the country. So I'll refer to them often in this book.

In 2015 the company implemented The Salesforce Moves 1,000,000 Mile Challenge to its employees. It worked so well to get their employees moving that in 2016 they bumped it up to 2,000,000 miles. And the company doesn't just offer this challenge to help with wellness. The Indianapolis location helps employees achieve their goals by offering treadmill desks and a fitness center in the same building.

But what if you're an office worker at a small company or one that just isn't offering a wellness program currently? You can sneak in small amounts of exercise that will add up to big results by:

1. Parking further away from your building to increase your walking each day.
2. Taking the stairs as much as possible versus the elevator.
3. If you work in an office, stand while you work. As I write this I am dictating into my tablet with it resting on a music stand. In this way, I can be on my feet and do some pacing as I write, which definitely burns more calories than sitting. I want to encourage you to talk to your employer about the possibility of a standing desk. But what if your company can't or won't pay for it? As I write this, there is a fabulous, inexpensive option on Amazon for only $25. It's made out of cardboard. When I researched this desk for my coworker Clarissa a couple of years ago, I didn't believe it would work. But as you'll see from the online reviews, people love it!
4. Take a 20-minute walk outside on your lunch hour. Yes, even in cold weather. In fact you burn more calories this way because your body is working harder to stay warm. Unless there are horrific wind chills, you won't freeze to death in 20 minutes as long as you're dressed appropriately. And as a bonus, a lunchtime walk will help you avoid the afternoon slump and keep you alert and productive after lunch.
5. If you're an early bird, walk with a family member, friend, or neighbor before work each morning. This also helps you be accountable since you know someone else will be waiting for you every day.

6. If you're more like me, you can take a walk after dinner three or four times a week. This is especially great if you have small children who can be pushed along in a stroller. It's wonderful bonding time and beneficial for all of you.

I've talked a lot about walking, and I encourage you to try to do at least a little of it each day since it's one of the easiest ways to get moving. But maybe walking's not your thing. Which leads me to my next point. If you're not currently exercising, you have to do some thinking and research to find the exercise you love. Once you find your "thing," you will make it a priority to find the time to do it at least two or three times a week. And that's enough to see some outstanding benefits for your health.

I found one of my "things" by accident. For as long as I can remember, I've always loved to dance. But typical exercises like aerobics and Zumba didn't excite me. A friend of mine talked to me about hoop dancing in the fall of 2010. Hoop dancing is basically what it sounds – dancing with a hula-hoop. The idea intrigued me, but as a busy working wife and mother, I never got around to exploring it. While on vacation visiting my sister in Florida in the spring of 2011, I watched some hoop dancers at a drum circle on the beach. I instantly fell in love and the next thing I knew I was giving a gal $20 to purchase a beginner adult hoop. I've been addicted ever since. In fact, when I haven't hoop danced in a few days, I start to get cranky and sluggish.

So how do you discover what exercise you'll stick with? Think back to your childhood. What sorts of things did you enjoy doing? Were you involved in any sports? Did you like swimming? Bicycling? These memories will give you some clues to what types of exercises you'd enjoy now. For example, I always loved walking my dog as a teenager and taking long walks on campus when I attended IU. I'm not surprised that I walk nearly every day now.

If you still don't have any ideas, you could always try various exercises for a short time to see if you like them. Many parks and recreation departments give local residents the opportunity to explore different programs for a short time at a low cost. The Field's Corner Parks Department has offered a "Try It Before You Buy It" in the past where people can try out a class before they pay for it. They've offered programs such as yoga, social dancing, Pilates, kickboxing, and much more.

It all goes back to starting small. Begin by doing whatever exercise you enjoy for 10 minutes each day or even every other day. Chances are you'll start to increase your time and your enjoyment and stay on the path to success!

If you still have some doubts about how exercise can change all aspects of your life after reading this, I encourage you to Google "100 benefits of exercise." The results are definitely motivating. And if you already have a job that involves a lot of physical activity and you're all set in the exercise category, good for you!

Please, before starting any exercise program, talk to your doctor about your plans to make certain they are right for you.

Now we'll move onto the next step to being healthier and feeling more joyful.

Eating Right

Notice that I didn't title this section "Diet." After so many years of use, this word has gained a negative connotation. I think it's better instead to say that we want to focus on eating the right foods, at least 80 percent of the time, in order to be healthy and feel good. Notice also that I didn't say we're going to focus on losing weight. If that's something you want to achieve, there are hundreds if not thousands of articles, books, and programs you can research and try. Not to mention it's important to once again speak to your doctor.

To put it simply, we have to eat well in order to feel good. I didn't grow up doing this. I remember eating a full bag of regular sized tortilla chips on occasion; consuming 2-3 glasses of soda almost every day (always with lots of ice, my favorite); devouring so many slices of pizza at times that it left my sister and brother-in-law in shock when I went out to eat with them; and sometimes eating two hamburgers for dinner.

My eating habits didn't change much when I was in my 20s, although being on my own meant I didn't have as much money to spend on food. Thankfully I've always had a good metabolism, so I've never been overweight. But I finally got my wake up call in my early 30s after having two children. My husband and I flew out to Nebraska for my niece's wedding in 2004 along with our two young sons. When I went to put on the dress that I had brought for the occasion, I was surprised to discover I couldn't zip it up. Thankfully I had brought another dress that actually fit, but it really bothered me that I couldn't wear what I wanted that day. That's when I realized something had to change.

If you already watch what you eat and feel good because of it, awesome! You can merrily skip to the next section of this chapter. For the rest of us, here is the number one way to help us be successful in eating right.

Once Again, Start Small

Are you sensing a theme here? I firmly believe a variety of small steps taken gradually are better than trying to do great big things all at once when it comes to eating healthier. Don't believe me? Look at how many people resolve to go on a diet and lose weight each year and how a large percentage of them fail. They set these huge unattainable goals involving a complete overhaul of everything that they do and it's just too overwhelming and often impossible.

The American Diabetes Association says the same thing. They encourage people to take small steps to change eating and exercise habits in order to prevent Type II Diabetes.

This is exactly how I began to eat better. It took me around two years to make the switches, reductions, or additions to my eating plan to get me to where I am today. And I am not perfect, nor should anyone be. Countless nutritionists, fitness experts, and medical professionals will tell you that if you never allow yourself the occasional treat, you will feel deprived and set yourself up for failure. And what fun would life be if you had to give up all those yummy things anyway? I mean, come on, can you imagine never again having a piece of pumpkin pie at Thanksgiving, a glass of eggnog at Christmas, or a truffle for Valentine's Day? That would be a tragedy. That's why I mentioned that whole "80 percent of the time" thing earlier and it's a rule I stick by. I eat healthy 80 percent of the time, and relax that rule around 20 percent of the time, especially on weekends and holidays.

So what are some small steps we can take to overhaul our eating habits? The following are some top tips from experts, many of which I've taken, that can be implemented gradually, one per month.

1. Drink more water and reduce soda and other sugary drinks. I'd love to say stop drinking soda and sugary drinks right away, but I know this is challenging, especially if your body is used to having soda with caffeine. Gradually reducing how much you consume will help you avoid the nasty side effects such as headaches and dizziness that people experience when they cut out these drinks cold turkey. And I still have orange juice and root beer myself once in awhile. But this first step can make you feel better quickly and rid your body of unnecessary calories, sugar, and/or toxins. Drinking more water helps increase your energy, makes you feel fuller before meals, helps your skin, and more. What if you find plain water unappealing and boring? You can drink tea as well, which is how I start my day. Coffee is also beneficial, although it's important to watch your caffeine intake. You can add a lot of things to water to give it some great flavor and sometimes more nutrition as well. For example, RachelRay.com writer Emily Wyckoff posted "10 Ways to Jazz Up Water" in May 2012.[13] If you look this up, you'll see that with various fruits, herbs, or even vegetables, you can make some great tasting water. My favorite is adding lemon slices to water, and most restaurants can accommodate this request.
2. Eat one small dessert a day, and make it a great one. A good friend of mine laughed when I told her about this one, but I used to eat two or three desserts a day and not think a thing about it, especially around holidays and celebrations when

we had pitch-ins at work. It was easy to have a cookie as a mid-morning snack, some ice cream after lunch, and cake after dinner. And sometimes this wasn't even stuff that I liked that much. I just ate it because it was there. I have a feeling I'm not alone. Now that I've gone down to just one small dessert a day that I really love, I've cut out tons of sugar and I look forward to a decadent little sweet treat. I've seen conflicting studies and reports on this idea, and some say that you should just enjoy one dessert a week. If you could be that disciplined, wonderful. But for me, having that one itty-bitty bit of heaven each day, especially at lunchtime when I can easily burn those calories off in the afternoon and evening, works well.

3. Eat more fruits and veggies and less crap. Duh. You knew this one was coming. And I'm not even going to bother to tell you why because we've all heard this from the time we were toddlers. But I am going to tell you how to make this easier. Let's tackle veggies first, which I think are harder and less tempting for most of us to eat. With vegetables, just remember two things: you can hide them in a lot of stuff and find fun ways to make them delicious. When you Google how to sneak veggies into your food, you'll be amazed at the results. Most of them are not hard and they are inexpensive. I personally love inspiralized.com. This ingenious site tells you how to make numerous vegetables into noodles that are absolutely delicious. Second, you can actually have fun making vegetables delicious. Find a healthy dip you enjoy that you can combine with fresh cut-up vegetables. Research some inventive salad ideas (but watch out for gobs of cheese, croutons, and other calorie-laden ingredients.) Go

online and discover some recipes for mouth-watering vegetable dishes. Have you ever roasted vegetables in the oven? Add some olive oil and some veggie grill seasoning and, oh my goodness, yum! It's a side dish my teenagers devour in minutes.

I think eating more fruits is easier for most of us because they contain sugar. My number one tip in this category is to mix things up. Try fruits you've never even heard of before from your local farmers market or grocery store. For instance, I have recently fallen in love with mango. It's almost like candy to me. I often substitute it and other fruits for the desserts I used to have all the time. Many fruits are portable and easy to snack on at your desk or when you are on the go at work.

1. Go nuts. This one makes me laugh because for most of my life I avoided nuts at all cost. I just didn't like them, especially with yummy Doritos® around. But by gradually trying different nuts and reducing the junk food (like those triangular chips that I used to snack on) I enjoy them and now feel fuller at snack time thanks to their fat and protein. Just watch your quantity, as most of the time a small handful is a serving, and add a little something sweet if you need to like dried cranberries, raisins, or a small square of dark chocolate. My 11 a.m. snack is a handful of almonds with a piece of dark chocolate and it keeps me going until lunch.
2. Watch those bedtime snacks. I went to the extreme on this one and learned it was not a good idea. Like many of us, I grew up eating a snack before I went to bed. But I learned

that you don't burn a ton of calories while you sleep, so I cut them out completely when I was in my 30s. Then I would lie awake in bed because I was hungry. And losing sleep is a no-no when we want to be positive in life (and something we'll discuss later on in this chapter.) Now my rule is to simply gauge my hunger in the evenings. If I'm not hungry before bed, I don't snack. But if my stomach is a little grumbly, I'll have a healthy low calorie snack. Men's Health has an excellent November, 2017 article discussing how to tell if you're truly hungry at this time of night and what sorts of snacks you should have a couple hours before going to bed.[14]

3. Reduce the white stuff, baby. This is another tip I'm sure you've read before. Mayo Clinic News reports that reducing consumption of white bread, rice, potatoes, and pasta and replacing them with whole-grain substitutes is a huge step in improving your health.[15] The "white stuff" increases your cravings for sugar, which makes you eat more and gets you into a vicious cycle. Fortunately, finding better alternatives is now easier than ever before. And my 80/20 rule applies once again in this step. For example, my kids refuse to eat anything but white hamburger buns. That's OK. Every other bread in our house is typically whole grain, which they don't mind. And white potatoes do offer some nutritional value. Just don't have them with each and every meal.

Those were just six of the dozens of ways you can take small steps to improve your meals and snacks to eventually enjoy healthier eating, which will translate to a healthier body. When I go the opposite way and indulge in some junk food or a heavy lunch, I find that I am more sluggish and not as productive at work. It's harder to be my joyful self.

So now that we've talked about some ways to exercise better and eat right, will move on to the #1 way to ensure we continue to do both of these every day - and this is the hardest thing for many of us.

Please Get Your Sleep

It seems like we can't go anywhere without seeing the topic of sleep addressed. It's in the news almost every week. At least one magazine in the checkout lanes each month at most grocery, dollar, or drug stores features an article about how to get more quality sleep. One thing is obvious – as a nation, many of us are not getting the sleep we need to be healthy and happy. Why? The Sleep Health Foundation gives these top 10 reasons:[16]

1. Taking sleep for granted and not thinking it is important.
2. Too much caffeine, alcohol, and sleeping tablets.
3. Shift work.
4. Jet lag.
5. Eating and drinking late.
6. Failing to wind down before bedtime.
7. Stress.
8. Sleep disorders.
9. Other medical conditions and pregnancy (and I'm going to add after pregnancy - we all know how babies keep people up at night!)
10. Drug side effects.

Fortunately there's a lot of information, resources, and medical professionals available to help people combat these problems, and great information about how to help your baby sleep through the night after a couple of months. And I beg you - if you are having trouble with your sleep, please do all you can to seek out solutions. This goes beyond being alert enough to be a positive person and to bring joy to your workplace. In addition to taking away any desire for you to exercise and eat healthy, a consistent lack of sleep can lead to some serious issues such as heart disease, stroke, depression, and diabetes.

On the reverse side, the right amount and quality of sleep can boost our immunity and reduce inflammation in the body. It helps us stay emotionally healthy and improves our social interactions.

I'm a highly sensitive person (yes, it's a real trait) and I don't function well after a night of poor sleep, especially at work. This doesn't happen to me very often, but when it does occur, I walk out the door at the end of the day feeling like I didn't do my best. Sleep is and always has been one of the keys to maintaining my enthusiasm. I know you'll find it's critical for you as well.

Give a Little, Get a Lot

Volunteering and helping others is a fantastic way to stay positive and productive at work. Salesforce believes in this and they prove it by giving their employees seven paid days for volunteering each year. The company says that volunteering is a part of its Ohana culture. This is a Hawaiian concept that means family. We'll talk more about this unique corporate culture in a later chapter.

Joy to You and Me (At Work!)

Fortune.com stated in April 2016 that giving workers paid time off to volunteer helps companies succeed.[17] It makes employees feel more connected and committed to their companies. Volunteering together also strengthens coworker relationships.

If you don't get paid to volunteer somewhere, I would still encourage you to donate just a few hours of your time each week or month to an organization that lights your fire. I know this can be challenging, especially if you are a working parent. Getting the whole family involved can help and can teach your children good values. Even toddlers can assist with projects such as a community garden or serving food to needy families. And you absolutely do get more than what you give. For example, I was so pleased last summer when my youngest son Jacob asked, "Can we do this again?" after we spent an evening with homeless families at our church. He loved seeing the reactions of the children when he played with them and wanted to bring smiles to their faces again.

On a basic level, I think helping others just gets us out of our own little pity parties. On a work day where I've let the little things get me down, I often force myself to take a break, get moving, look around, and see where someone might need some help or cheer. This always helps me put things in perspective and remember that I'm not the only one in the world with problems. I typically return to my tasks with a renewed sense of hope and enthusiasm afterwards.

Talk to the Big Guy… or the Universe… or Whoever/Whatever

I had to end this chapter with this suggestion because it's at the very center of my being and probably the number one reason why I'm so joyful. I'm talking about prayer here, Folks. I know not everyone believes in God or a god, but it sure helps me get through each and every day. If you don't believe in anything like that, there's always chatting with the Universe.

Mr. Carnegie calls prayer or talking to any sort of higher power the "perfect way to conquer worry." I believe it's the reason I'm alive and well. Before I took Mr. Carnegie's class, worry consumed my life. In fact I was a pro at it. I've been to the emergency room twice due to chest pains thanks to anxiety.

Of course there are numerous ways to conquer worry and stress, and Mr. Carnegie has 29 other suggestions you can review. But for me, prayer is quick and sometimes immediately helpful. When those awful moments hit and you feel like you want to explode on the job, sometimes a ten-minute walk while you mentally send your problems out to the universe can do wonders.

I worked with an amazing, spunky lady named Liz years ago at a therapeutic horseback-riding center just northeast of Indianapolis. Whenever any one of us was stressed or worried, she would quietly ask, "Did you Philippians 4:6 it?" She was referring to the passage in the Bible that starts out by essentially saying "Don't worry about anything, but pray about everything." It's a statement I still use to this day and it greatly eases my burdens both in and out of the workplace.

Ready. Set. Go!

I hope you've been able to jot down at least a few new ideas throughout this chapter to help you be your healthiest, happiest self. You'll already be an example of joy to everyone you know and meet just by adopting some of these habits. Are you ready to wow them even more? Let's go!

"You never get a second chance to make a good first impression." *Will Rogers*

Chapter Four

Everyday Ways to Be Joyful

Now it's time for us to get down to some serious joyful business. And the good news is that a lot of these tips you can start doing today to pleasantly surprise your coworkers and customers. To begin, let's work on some first impressions.

Bring Your Voicemail Greeting Out of Snoozeville

We've all heard and many of us have recorded that same old voicemail greeting. You know what I'm talking about. "This is Joe Schmoe with the ABC Company. I'm either out of the office or away from my desk right now. Please leave your name, number, and a brief message and I'll return your call as soon as possible. Thank you." I'm almost asleep as I write this. This is Snoozeville at its finest and certainly not the happiest of greetings.

Our voicemail message is one of the first impressions we give others on the job. Shouldn't we make it stand out to show customers and remind fellow employees how awesome we are as well as our company? Of course, we have to make certain it is appropriate for the work that we do. No one wants to hear an overly chipper greeting if they're calling, for example, a funeral home! When in doubt about your greeting, be sure to talk to a supervisor.

If you have the freedom to be a little creative, go for it! Start with these tips from driventoexcel.com:[18]

1. Script, rehearse, and then record. It's tempting to rush through your message or to just get your greeting over with. But you want to give directions to your caller and to sound confident. By taking a little time and effort, you'll avoid saying those annoying little "Uhs" and "Ums" and be crystal clear.
2. Smile. It's been said that people can tell when you're smiling on the phone. I even stand a lot of times when I record a voicemail greeting. By both smiling and standing, you project positive energy into your message that your caller will pick up on instantly.
3. Be brief, informative, positive, and upbeat. You can skip a lot of extra information nowadays, such as saying "After the tone please leave your message," and "I'm sorry I'm away from my desk right now." Most everyone knows to wait for the beep, and they also realize you can't be near your phone 24/7. Instead, you can leave helpful information for your caller such as your website address, an alternate phone number, or a way to bypass the voicemail greeting altogether to quickly leave a message.
4. Take the opportunity to leave pertinent information. Maybe you're a salesperson and on the road often and can only return calls at a specific time each day. Perhaps your company has relocated. Here's a great chance to take a couple of seconds to let your callers know this vital info.

I'll throw in my own two cents and encourage you to please record your own voicemail. It's strange to call someone and hear a totally different person say, "Mr. Smith is away from his desk right now." Unless you're mute, have a horrible voice, or you're the President of the United States, I hope you'll consider recording your own greeting. It makes a world of difference and shows your confidence.

I currently work for Link Observatory Space Science Institute, which is just as cool as it sounds. Here is my greeting:

"Hello, you've reached the voicemail box of Amy Shankland with Link Observatory Space Science Institute (slight pause) - exploring the wonders of the universe! Please leave your name, number, and a brief message and I'll return your call just as soon as possible. Thanks."

Notice I don't give my title. I wear a variety of hats for the organization, so I don't necessarily want to say that I am a sales person or the development manager to avoid confusion on the caller's part. You may need to put in your title, but in just six words I sum up what we do to make it clear to the caller - exploring the wonders of the universe. It often piques peoples' interest. When our director first heard this message, he complimented me on it and said he was inspired to change his own!

You can actually make someone's day or motivate them with your voicemail. You want people to hang up and think, "Wow, that's someone I'd love to talk to." I encourage you to definitely get out of the box on this one. If you work for a more relaxed company, add a touch of appropriate humor.

Yes, it takes a little extra time, but with a well-thought-out voicemail you'll get a lot in return, such as more business, giving a coworker a much-needed laugh, or maybe a great compliment from your boss!

Amy Thornton

Make Your Email Signature Come Alive

I love how email has evolved in recent years. It's great that you can add your picture or one that represents who you are or what your company does. And with social media so popular, having a picture and some extras in our emails makes a lot of sense. People are used to more and more visuals in communication now. But most of us spend less time on our email signatures than our voicemails. However, this is another opportunity to make a strong first impression.

Your department or company may want all email signatures to be similar, perhaps including a logo, website, social media channels, office number, disclaimer, etc. The Link Institute is the same way. But I can still personalize my email with a nice headshot. And instead of saying "Warm Regards" or "Yours Truly" at the end, for years I've written "With Enthusiasm" before my name. Anyone who knows me says it sums me up perfectly. Heck, if you like it I'll even let you borrow it for your own email signature!

My former boss at the county soil and water conservation district had a beautiful picture of a drop of water bouncing and leaving ripples in her email signature. She definitely captured what we did and it illustrates the saying "A picture is worth a thousand words." Another coworker named Cindy always signed her emails, "Serving Joyfully." This reflected her personality beautifully.

Maybe you have some leeway and you can explore different fonts and colors for your email signature. Or perhaps you'd just like a little help in this area because you're short on time. You can try one of these three email signature generators: WiseStamp, NewOldStamp, or htmlsig.

No matter what direction you choose, follow the same guidelines as with voicemail. Be positive, be brief, and only give pertinent information. For example, it's not necessary to put your email address at the bottom of the message, since people can just hit "reply" to get it. But your email signature might be a great opportunity to provide a link for your latest promotion, such as an annual native tree sale if you work for a soil and water conservation district. With a little thought and effort, your signature could bring you and your company more benefits than you ever imagined and show the world your positive attitude.

Make your Surroundings Uplifting

If you have an office, cubicle, desk, corner, or some little world inside your company that is your very own, you need to make that space as uplifting as possible. If you spend a lot of time in a vehicle for your job, you need to make it a pleasant atmosphere. Why? It makes a big difference in your mood and energy day after day. Think back to all that time you spend at work that we talked about in the introduction. Do you really want to spend a little less than half of your waking hours in a drab, draining, messy environment?

There really is something to feng shui, the Chinese philosophy about working to be in harmony with your environment. Unfortunately this term was over-used years ago and when it's said now it sometimes produces eye rolls. But it's not as wonky as some people think. Real Simple magazine interviewed Catherine Brophy, feng shui master and interior designer, who said that the purpose of feng shui is to get your environment in line with who you are and where you want to go.[19] I think this makes perfect sense on the job.

You have to take care of the basics first, and that's making certain your area is organized and de-cluttered. A good feng shui practice is to make certain 50 percent of your desk is clear. An atmosphere of chaos makes it difficult to be productive. It's been said over and over that a cluttered desk equals a cluttered mind. For many of us, having our desk completely uncluttered is impossible or simply won't work for what we do. But I believe most of us can handle getting it down to 50 percent

Another important point is to face a door or other opening if you have that option. Feng shui says having your back to a door or window weakens your energy. But if you think that's all baloney, let's move instead to common sense. What would you rather look at all day, a wall, furniture, or some open space? Besides, it's better for people to walk into your area and see your face rather than your back.

You may not have that option. Perhaps you're in a cubicle or you have shared desk space. You can still take some steps to brighten up your environment. In fact, your cubicle can be absolutely fabulous with some effort and creativity. I highly recommend the book *Cube Chic* by Kelley L. Moore, available on Amazon.[20] Moore is a lifestyle and entertaining expert with a mission to empower people to connect and build relationships through the environment they create. This fun book can help you transform those three gray walls into something you'll look forward to working in. It can be your own positive space that others will be drawn to. Moore has photographs, instructions, and material lists showing how to create 22 different themes for your office space. They range from Safari, to Glam, Golf, Casino, Zen, Sci-fi, and more. The ideas are quite elaborate, and require a variety of materials as well as a good glue gun.

You may be thinking, "No way. I don't have time to work with a glue gun and totally transform my cubicle. I have a life." And that is completely understandable. However, her book can inspire you to do *some* things to bring changes to your workspace. At least it can get the wheels turning to show you some great themes and possibilities.

Sarah Ban Breathnach, author of the New York Times bestseller, *Simple Abundance,* talks about how we need to create brief daily rituals to help us feel calm and ready to tackle or end the day. She encourages us to set aside 10 minutes each day before it officially begins to enjoy a cup of coffee, tea, cocoa, etc. Breathnach suggests ending the day by straightening up our desks and reviewing the next day's agenda. It might be challenging to find this time, but even five minutes can help set the stage for joy and productivity.

She says we all need a work drawer or locker with items to make the day positive, like mints, tissues, aspirin, or even some grown-up toys for when we just need to get away from being adults for a minute like a yo-yo or Silly Putty. For example, it's hard for me to sit still during a phone conference or a webinar, so I like to keep something nearby for me to occupy my hands while I stand and listen. Keeping my hands moving helps me focus during these sometimes hour-long sessions.

Breathnach also talks about aromatherapy. Diffusers will not only make our work environment smell good, but they can put moisture back into the air, which is also helpful in heated offices. The scent can either be soothing or invigorating depending on what you need to do your best. Once again, be sensitive to your coworkers. Make certain whatever you are thinking of using will help them as well, not irritate them. Some people are bothered by certain fragrances, or have allergies.

What about the temperature of your workspace? I almost hesitate to write about this because I know in recent years it has become a hot button (pun intended), especially for women. As I type, thousands if not millions of space heaters are running in work spaces around the country - and the world - 365 days a year, whether they're supposed to or not. It's challenging to find the right temperature for everyone. Women have lower metabolic rates than men and tend to have more body fat, so they are typically more susceptible to cold. Weight and age can affect sensitivity to temperatures as well. Leaders in the workplace need to consider factors such as building design and who makes up their workforce when determining temperatures. It's difficult for people to be positive and productive when they are either too hot or too cold.

Unfortunately there is no easy solution on this one. I've seen varying studies on what experts believe is the ideal workplace temperature. Many of them say between 71 and 72°F is perfect. But I know my husband and several of my male friends would be sweating profusely at this temperature.

There is hope. The Wall Street Journal said in a March 2017 article that new technologies are giving individual workers more control on the climate around them.[21] Modern tech company AppNexus has 27 offices. Managers used to hear a variety of complaints about office temperatures, which became quite stressful at times, without easy solutions other than adjusting the work zones of those who complained the most. Then the company installed Comfy[22], where employees could adjust the air around their desk with an app. It worked well, especially after AppNexus offered the Comfy Challenge where people who used the app the most received prizes every month. The system wasn't perfect, but it was a vast improvement and freed up managers' time to do other, more important tasks.

    I'm one of those cold people. My number one strategy through the years has been to wear layers, especially when I used to walk back-and-forth to work. It's not the perfect solution, but it's a good option for people who work in places that don't have advanced technology like AppNexus. I think it's important for employees to keep respectfully talking to one another and to work with their leaders to find the best compromise for this problem.

    Incorporating beautiful, colorful art and photographs is another wonderful way to make your surroundings positive. When I went from an office with windows at the Town of Field's Corner to something that was more of a closet, I bought brightly - colored lamps, coat hooks, and inexpensive art from thrift stores. I hung scenes from nature on my wall to make me think of the outdoors. And I purchased a couple of hardy plants that grew well in a typical office's harsh lighting. They actually lived during their 18 months in that space, a huge accomplishment for me!

    Plants, by the way, bring both beauty and health benefits to most any workspace. They purify the air, which is important to battle the common office indoor air pollution. Gardening Know How says they can even help reduce stress.[23] Make certain to select varieties that don't require a lot of care, such as spider plants, philodendrons, and peace lilies.

What if all you have as far as your own personal space at work is a locker? You can certainly have fun with that as well. Most of us had a locker in middle or high school, and some of us have one at our local gym. This is where Pinterest comes in handy! Even HGTV and Buzz Feed have guidance on sprucing up a locker. And what's great here is that you can do whatever the heck you want as long as it's legal! Once that locker door is shut, no one has to know about your video game, unicorn, kitten, football, or other themed decor. You can go wild with that space and make it something you look forward to seeing in the morning, on a break, or before you leave.

What if your "office" is a vehicle? AllTrucking.com estimates that there are 3.5 million truck drivers in the United States today.[24] Many salespersons and people who drive for Uber, Lyft, and other ride sharing services spend lots of hours in their cars. I think it's even more important to have a joyful atmosphere for these scenarios. It doesn't just make *you* feel better, but it helps increase your business.

My husband John has been driving for Uber for over two months now. His father taught him that if you do a job, always strive to do it well. John makes certain his car is neat, clean, and de-cluttered inside and out. He uses an air freshener that's not overpowering. He added a bag that hangs on the back of the front passenger seat that contains small bottles of water and mints. John bought some hand cream in the winter for people to use to combat the dry air. He set up a contraption to hold his iPad behind the driver's seat and has it locked so passengers can play a trivia game while they ride to pass the time. John took these steps after conducting research about what successful drivers do and he also thought about what he would like as a passenger. John wants his customers to have the best Uber experience.

By doing all of this, people are saying they want to request him! John has consistently received five star ratings from passengers who take the time to rate drivers.

John doesn't just do all of this for his customers - he does it for himself. He is a salesman for his full-time position and travels throughout Central Indiana each day. John is convinced that all of this effort helps him stay positive for himself as well as his customers.

Hopefully by now you understand just how important it is to make your workspace come alive for yourself, your coworkers, and potentially your customers. You may also be totally freaking out, wondering how you'll find the time to transform your little world, especially if your space is messy and cluttered. This is when we go back to those small steps, People. Perhaps the first month you focus on the top of your desk. The following month you can work on creating a better system for filing papers. Then you can eventually move on to the fun stuff like finding art, photographs, or other decor. And you don't have to spend a lot of money. Some of my favorite finds are from my local St. Vincent de Paul thrift store. This makes them unique as well!

I want to encourage you to keep your eye on the prize as you work toward your goal. Breathnach states that authentic success involves feeling focused and serene when you work, not fragmented. I know that's not always possible every hour of every day, and it certainly has not always been the case for me. But it's a goal we all should strive to reach as often as we can.

Sketch out or write down how you want your workspace to look and feel, map out a plan to achieve that goal in six months or even a year, and think of the peace and joy you'll feel whenever you're in or around it every day. It's worth it.

Don't Ignore that Computer, Tablet, Laptop, etc.

I've seen statistics saying that Americans are on a screen anywhere from 5 to 10 hours a day. A lot of that screen time is for work purposes. Many of us work with a computer, laptop, tablet, or other mobile device for our professions. Some are just using mobile devices only. In fact, according to a 2016 article in ComScore, computer usage is falling, as 20 percent of millennials strictly use mobile devices.[25] No matter what you use, you want to make certain to apply some of the same principles that we talked about for your physical work environment.

Are your computer files and documents well organized so it's easy to find what you need? How does your email look? Do you have hundreds of messages in your inbox vs. organized into folders? Do you have a good system for saving documents other than throwing them on your desktop (shudder)?

De-cluttering your device is essential. It may be even more essential then de-cluttering your desk or other physical workspace, as most of us are getting away from using paper and instead keeping more electronic documents. There are a lot of ways you can organize your files, and I won't go into all of the methods here. Techlicious, Microsoft, Huffington Post, and many other companies have great articles online that you can research to discover the system that works for you. Different people have different ways of thinking, so you have to match your work style to the appropriate system.

Once you organize the inside of your device, make sure the outside looks good. Are you one of those sticky note people who like to plaster the perimeter of their screen with reminders? I'm talking about the actual paper, not the program you can use in your device - from what I can see the Sticky Note program for your computer might be quite useful! At one time I did use paper notes like a picture frame around my desktop to try to help me remember things. By doing this, I had too many notes that almost blurred together and they never helped me remember a thing!

I personally love to use a combination of phone alarms and Outlook to remind me of appointments and tasks. Some friends of mine still use good old paper planners. Once again, you have to know what works for you.

So once you've organized your computer or device inside and out, what do you see when you first log in every day? Is it still the default wallpaper that came with the computer? That will take you quickly back into Snoozeville territory. Joyful employees don't hang out there.

Since you're looking at this device for several hours each day, why not make it something motivating, beautiful, or inspiring? Or cute. You can't go wrong with cute, unless it's too cute for a professional environment. Your computer or device probably already has wallpapers you can choose from. If you don't like any of those, there are thousands of options that are easy to download from the Internet.

I've always enjoyed having a current picture of my two sons as the wallpaper for my work computer. I have a picture of our pets as the background for my iPad, and another picture of my boys for my phone. Of course I get busy and don't always take the time to appreciate these pictures, but once in a while when things get chaotic, it's nice to take a moment and see the ones I love. They remind me why I do what I do.

The Sound of Music

Music is one of my passions and probably one of the top things I use in order to stay joyful. I grew up playing the piano, clarinet, and some percussion. I've also sung in my church choir. I hoop dance to it to get my blood pumping and put me in a meditative state. Our whole family enjoys a variety of genres of music. Like many people, it can move me and make me feel a myriad of emotions.

It's no wonder that I, like many people, often work at my computer while listening to music. Entrepreneur.com states that, when used strategically, music can increase your productivity.[26] In a noisy open office environment, slipping on some headphones or putting in ear buds can help you focus better on your tasks. Music is especially helpful when you have to complete a repetitive project such as entering data into a spreadsheet. The site goes on to say that you want to listen to familiar songs or ambient music so you can focus better throughout the day.

What if you're on your feet with a more physically demanding job? Even better! For years my husband John was in the bicycle retail and repair business. This meant he was on his

Joy to You and Me (At Work!)

feet for an average of 10 hours a day. Listening to music helped motivate him and his friends when they were doing repairs in the back of the shop, and often helped them stay awake and focus on the task at hand. It also led to some laughter and raised eyebrows when customers would find them dancing as they worked!

Speaking of retail, music can help not just employees, but customers as well. The City of Noblesville partnered with Noblesville Main Street years ago to start playing music over loudspeakers throughout its historic downtown district during the holidays. Main Street leads the efforts to develop and promote the downtown and its surrounding areas. The reason for this change? The partners knew that the right music can put people in good moods, create a brand for a store or shopping area, attract customers, and increase sales and revenue. I currently serve on the Noblesville Main Street board and the director, Chris, told me he regularly receives positive feedback about the city providing music. On Small Business Saturday, Chris shared that several shoppers commented on the festive nature of downtown with its music and carolers.

What if you're not a "music" person? As hard is it is for many of us to understand, some people just don't derive pleasure from it. I'm good friends with someone like this and she is one of the sweetest people I know. So we music people have to respect non-music people (and vice versa!). This is where those headphones and ear buds come in quite handy.

White noise, which is similar to a fan running, can be helpful in this situation. When I was temporarily covering for a department at Field's Corner, I had to sit in the quiet front reception area where the town manager didn't want music playing. Without having a fan running, this would have been torture, as it has always been difficult for me to work in total silence. It's especially challenging now that I have tinnitus, or a ringing, in my right ear. Thankfully with the world we live in, this rarely bothers me, as most of us don't encounter total silence very often.

White noise is also helpful in a shared office space. According to the University of Sydney, white noise and its relatives, pink and brown noises, can help mask sounds and increase concentration.[27] I use pink noise thanks to an app on my iPad at night to block out the tinnitus and help me sleep. I like using an app rather than a fan because sometimes I don't want my room to be cooler, such as in the winter. There are many apps out there that are free or low-cost to help you experiment with different soothing sounds to help your workspace be more pleasant and productive. You may want to work together with others in your shared space to find the right combination for everyone.

I encourage you to experiment with either music or white noise to find the right formula to help soothe, motivate, and move you to do your joyful best!

What's Up With That Wardrobe?

Okay, so you are on your way to creating a joyful workspace with wonderful sights, sounds, temperatures, and perhaps aromas. Your voicemail and email make people happy. There's just one more frontier for us to conquer – our work wardrobes. Dressing for success not only helps us move up the ladder in our companies, but it helps us feel positive. The Wall Street Journal stated in February of 2016 that research shows when workers wear nicer clothes, they achieve more.[28]

I must admit I failed in this category miserably years ago when I worked from home after my first son was born. I dressed terribly. Perhaps it was a combination of being a new mother, dealing with the occasional lack of sleep, and juggling work with a new baby that caused it. And forget about makeup or doing my hair. When I look back at photos from that time period, I see that my "uniform" was a ponytail, no makeup, a t-shirt, and shorts or sweatpants. And, God forbid, Mom Jeans - the subject of Saturday Night Live skits and other satirical scenarios. If you don't know what Mom Jeans are, let's just say they are less than flattering.

Sadly, things didn't change much after the birth of my second son, especially when I ran a home daycare for a couple of years. Somehow I pulled myself together and dressed well for my interview for the Town of Field's Corner and returned to the typical office setting in early 2007. Thankfully, a combination of an illness and fate led me to binge watch the former popular TLC show "What Not to Wear" soon after I started. This show opened my eyes to how a person's dress can affect his or her performance on the job.

Perhaps you have to wear a uniform for work, so this is not an issue for you. Love it or hate it, a uniform simplifies the whole "what to wear" dilemma and gives everyone a unified appearance. I created my own uniform when I worked for the soil and water conservation district. We were allowed to wear casual to business casual attire, so I bought different colored polo shirts and the office paid to have a logo embroidered on each one. It was nice not to think about what to wear each morning, as I typically would put on one of the polo shirts along with jeans or khakis.

Some people create a uniform in more formal office settings. In 2015, an art director shared in Harpers Bazaar how she bought numerous white silk blouses and black pants for her own day to day uniform. She added a blazer and accessories to change up the look. This art director's idea is nothing new. Men have essentially been wearing a uniform for decades – a suit. With more relaxed dress codes, both men and women are often wearing what I did at soil and water - polo shirts and khakis or pants. Creating our own uniform can free up time for us to focus on more important issues each day vs. thinking about what to wear.

For some, however, a uniform is boring and stifling. No matter what, dressing thoughtfully and with care affects your attitude and performance at work. I'm working from home once again, but this time I make certain to wear at least a bit of make up, have my hair in an actual style, and put on real clothes.

Remember, dressing well doesn't have to mean spending a lot of money. My dear friend Cora, the former public affairs director for the Town of Field's Corner, does an amazing job of dressing well, but has a knack for being frugal. Obviously it was of upmost importance for her to look polished and professional in this position, as she was representing the town and its employees every day. Cora pays attention to what fits her well and to what colors bring out her best features. Her favorite shops? TJ Maxx and garage sales!

You might be thinking, "I have no idea how to do that." Frankly, neither did I. But if I can change and dress better, anyone can. "What Not to Wear" helped me and countless other men and women, but the show is off the air now. There are plenty of resources out there to help you dress your best, including YouTube videos, department store ads, and personal stylists. Or just pick a well-dressed friend like Cora and see if he or she can give you some free advice!

Whether you have to wear a uniform, choose to create one, or embark on a journey to wear a variety of professional apparel, dressing well is an easy way to ensure you start your work with the right attitude.

Your Morning/Afternoon/Evening Greeting

How do you greet others when you begin your shift? Are you barely moving or barely alive? Do you at least smile and say, "Good morning/afternoon/evening"? Or is the thought of speaking to others when you begin to work absolutely dreadful for you?

As I've mentioned, I am not a morning person. I would rather start my day at 9:00 or 9:30 a.m. But most offices start the day at 8 o'clock in the morning and the Town of Field's Corner was no exception. Some work places are offering more flexible schedules nowadays, but this is still rare.

Thankfully my morning walks helped me wake up and transformed me into my joyful self. You may have to find your own routine to psych yourself up to greet others in a pleasant manner. Remember how we talked about acting enthusiastic to become enthusiastic? Some mornings even my walk wasn't enough, but once I announced, "Good Morning, Suite 275!" when I entered the town manager's suite, my mood and that of others who heard me was instantly uplifted. In fact, when I left the town when my position changed and no longer fit my skills, I bought a little white teddy bear and recorded that same greeting for my friend Maddy to listen to whenever she wanted. She loved it and offered me heartfelt thanks. It made me feel incredible to know that such a small gesture was making a difference in her life every morning.

A few people may not appreciate your positivity each day. My former boss who didn't like my personality was one of them. After awhile, he wouldn't permit me to say good morning or to ask how his evening or weekend went. But most people will appreciate a happy person and even if they don't feel the same way, they'll benefit from a positive ray of light to start the workday. And you'll feel your best as well!

Please, for the Love of All That is Holy Take a Break

Most of us are quite busy in our professions. Sometimes it can feel like there is no way we can possibly take ten minutes for lunch, let alone any other break in the day. But that's exactly what we should do in order to be as productive and happy as possible. Dale Carnegie said that it is important to rest before you get tired. His book *How to Stop Worrying and Start Living* shares many examples of how successful people are more productive because they allow themselves to take breaks.

I like to use an analogy to help people understand why this is so important. Let's think about a car. When a car starts to overheat, should we let it keep running or turn it off to let the engine cool down? Of course we need to do the latter. What about if it's low on fuel? Do we just keep driving and watch the warning light flash and the countdown of miles left until it's empty? Absolutely not. Unless we want to get stuck somewhere by the side of the road and go nowhere, we need to find the nearest gas station and refuel.

The same thing applies to human beings. Whether your job is physical or more sedentary, you're using energy in some way. Our bodies need the occasional rest or meal so we can keep going. Do you remember my friend Clarissa, the wonderful QuickBooks wizard? She's young, energetic, and a hard worker. Clarissa has run a marathon and several half marathons. But I still worried about her when we worked together because she always ate lunch at her desk. Clarissa rarely took a break and I would gently tease her about running out of steam. I even mentioned once that she seemed tired, often yawning throughout the day. Last fall, she started to change her habit of never taking a break and took real lunch hours, going outside as much as possible.

"It's very refreshing and helps me be invigorated for the rest of the day," she says. "It's like a refill! I try to at least go to the back table to eat and read if I can't go outside due to the cold."

And it's important not to just take breaks during your work time. Remember to take the occasional long weekend or vacation to get completely away for a while, even if you just take a "staycation" at home. Americans are terrible about taking the time off that they so desperately need. I've read various studies saying that more than half of us did not take all of our allotted vacation time in 2016. The reasons for this vary, including worry about returning to a mountain of work and the feeling that no one else can do the job. However, most managers will agree that vacation time helps with health and well-being, boosts morale, and alleviates burnout.

As counterintuitive as it is, in order to be joyful in our workplaces, we need to get away from them once in a while, whether it's an hour every day for lunch, or a couple of weeks a year for some much-deserved rest and relaxation. If this is a hard concept for you, build up to it gradually and see how you do. Challenge yourself to take at least a half hour to have a proper lunch away from your desk or main workspace every day. If it's been forever since you've had that vacation, look at your calendar and see if you can take a four-day weekend in the next 2 to 3 months. Later on, examine your mood and how well you accomplish your tasks when you try these steps. I'm confident you'll find that you'll be a more positive, energetic person because you allowed yourself to take the time to rest physically, mentally, and emotionally.

Smile Even If No One's Watching

Sometimes we just have to be our own little cheerleaders. My last tip in this section is probably the easiest thing to do, but it's also easy to forget. We gotta smile. It involves that "fake it 'til you make it" mentality. I'm not saying that we have to smile when something truly sad or upsetting is happening in our lives. Even I can't do that. But when we're having one of those "meh" days, sometimes putting that smile on our faces can help us sound and feel better when we're on the phone, interacting with customers, or encountering that often difficult coworker.

Let's smile and celebrate the little victories at work even when we're by ourselves! Why not do a little happy dance when we close that sale, impress our boss, get that raise or promotion, or put on a successful event? Sometimes no one else knows how hard we worked, so giving ourselves those silly rewards can mean a lot. Smile and celebrate the little things as much as possible and you will be a positive force to everyone around you in the workplace.

Part Two

How to Bring Joy to Your Co-Workers

Amy Thornton

"People don't care how much you know until they know how much you care" *Theodore Roosevelt (or one of dozens of other people this quote has been attributed to)*

Chapter Five

Why Should We Care About Making Co-Workers Happy?

Now that we are more joyful at work, or on our way to that goal, we can turn our attention to spreading joy to others. I can't even begin to tell you how much I love this part. Once you start to make even the occasional effort in your workplaces, you'll get big results and feel amazing at the same time.

Let's review why we want to spread joy to others at work. Sure, it's a nice thing to do and I believe it is the right thing to do, but there's so much more to it. The reasons we want our fellow employees to be joyful are, of course, similar to why *we* are working on being joyful people - they'll be more productive and experience less stress. I can't say they will be stress-free, because there's no magic formula for that. Every job involves some stress. But with the positive example you set and the joyful steps you are about to take, you'll help your fellow employees experience less stress and handle the difficult times much better.

It's just so gosh darn fun, too. Do you ever have that wonderful feeling of anticipation at Christmas time or when it's someone's birthday? When you absolutely positively know you got that person the most perfect gift in the universe and you just can't wait to see their reaction? That's how I feel every time I do something special for one of my co-workers. I take my life's mission quite seriously, folks!

Let's look at the quote that kicked off this chapter that's been attributed to dozens of people throughout the years. "People don't care how much you know until they know how much you care." No matter who the heck said it, it's the best way to illustrate why it's important not to just care about our work, but care about the ones doing that work along with us.

No one illustrates this better than Dan Walsh, one of my sons' former elementary school teachers. Mr. Walsh, as he is better known to thousands in the Central Indiana area, is a legend to his former students, the parents of those former students, and any faculty member who's ever had the privilege of working beside him. I'll put it this way - if there were a TV show called "America's Got Joy" instead of "America's Got Talent," all of the judges would advance him to the final round at first sight - and then he'd win in that round.

Mr. Walsh is now retired and shared with me in an interview that he believes in, making people feel important, validated, and not invisible. "Make others the star," is part of his philosophy. "People want to be seen and heard," he says. He emphasizes that if people don't feel recognized, they often get defensive. Mr. Walsh did a great job with recognizing others when he taught elementary school and I'll share one of his stories later on.

I have a feeling the opposite philosophy is one of the major reasons so many people are unhappy at work, which is why I wrote this book. An October 2012 article from Forbes states that when people have to exercise restraint, measure their words, and basically walk on eggshells around others, the result is poor workmanship, missed deadlines, and cracks in the company or department's culture.[29] This negativity can affect clients and customers and create turnover.

At a time when many of us are working more than 40 hours a week as mentioned in the beginning of this book, it can be challenging to remember to take time for others. But it's actually more important than ever before. Taking a moment here and there to build strong relationships at work creates high morale and actually leads to fun and increased productivity.

Showing how much you care can also ease potential tensions. My father-in-law, Ryan, was a great example of this before he retired. Ryan worked for a large company years ago making plastic bottles. Thanks to his observations that helped increase safety and decrease leakage in their systems, he was quickly promoted. Ryan was assigned to learn all about some new machinery and to create a manual for it so anyone could run it. He became a shift supervisor after only 2-1/2 months and was promoted ahead of others who have been there for years. But he always remembered where he came from.

Ryan gathered everyone together after his promotion and said, "They've chosen me to do this and I don't know why. You guys taught me what I know now. We can work together as a team and try to make things better or you can fight me." Thanks to his humility and honesty, everyone chose to work together - and later on, people were asking to join his crew! I'll tell you why in the next chapter.

No matter what your level is on the job, you can be a powerful force for change. Being a positive example at work is like the start of a ripple in a body of water - your bit of joy may be just a drop in the pond, but it can make circles and expand to all of its edges and reach so many.

Let's move on to the ways we can start bringing joy to others at work.

Amy Thornton

"Celebrate Good Times, C'mon!" *Kool and the Gang*

Chapter Six

Celebrate!

Birthdays. Administrative Professionals Day. Boss's Day. Christmas. Groundhog Day. Halloween. These are all occasions when we can do something special for others, recognize them on the job, or just simply dress up and look goofy for a day. Okay, maybe not necessarily Groundhog Day, although during a particularly tough, long winter it may be the perfect excuse for some fun.

The first thing I do when I start a new job is learn everyone's birthday in my company - or, if it's a large one, my department. It's easy to put the dates in an Outlook calendar and set a recurrence for a reminder to pop up every year. If you're more of a paper planner/calendar person, you can buy a perpetual calendar at a reasonable price - I've seen some for as low as $3 - so once you write down a birthday you'll always have it. I also make certain to highlight what months Boss's Day and Administrative Professional's Day fall in, since these dates change every year.

Once you've marked down everyone's birthdays or other special days and you get to know your co-workers a bit, it's time to plan! Let's start simply.

Cards

I think now more than ever, a real card means a lot to people. With most of our communication being done via email, social media, or text/call, getting a card stands out. You can go as elaborate or as simple as you like here. If you don't have a "party fund" where everyone contributes an amount they feel comfortable giving every year or every quarter for special occasions, you can make your own card. There are free templates and card makers online where you can create cards in just a few minutes.

If you do have a party fund or are able to buy cards for co-workers on your own, stock up on appropriate, fun cards the next time you visit a dollar store. I like to get cards to match various personalities. For example, my friend Cora was nicknamed The Princess when she worked for the Town of Field's Corner, so I was always on the lookout for any card with a tiara! If you don't know everyone quite yet, stay on the safe side and stick to themes like balloons, cake, candles, etc. I always make certain that I know someone fairly well before going into the "humorous card" territory. You also want to respect different cultures as well.

Next, create a checklist of names you can print off for each card-signing occasion. End the checklist with the phrase, "Last person to sign the card please return to Amy," or whatever your name is. I put this checklist in a brightly colored folder labeled, "Signature Needed," along with the card and place it on the first person's chair so he or she can easily see it. If you're not in an office, you can put the folder along with a pen in a hidden location in a common area such as the break room.

One important note - give people a lot of time to sign the card. I try to get the folder circulating at least the day before the special occasion if not sooner. You never know when someone might have a day off, a big project they have to complete, or an emergency. If someone's on vacation or ill, you can always sign their name and put, "Signature on File," - something we jokingly did at the Town of Field's Corner.

I always sign the card first to set the tone. Depending on how well I know the individual, I'll put a sincere compliment, "inside" (departmental) joke, or at least a comment about what a pleasure it is to work with the person.

Once you get the card back, now it's delivery time! You can tape it to the person's door or locker, leave it in their coat, on their chair, etc. I try to make it a surprise whenever possible, since most people love surprises. If you just can't make a surprise happen, there's nothing wrong with giving it to someone before lunch or at the end of their shift with a smile and a wish for a great day.

Most of the time, people aren't even getting many cards from their own family or circle of friends. This small gesture will make their day, week, or month!

Emails

In this day and age of telecommuting and other unique work situations, sometimes it's not possible for everyone to sign a card. That's the case with my current job where all six of us work from home around the Indianapolis area. We only get together every couple of months, and then we're often busy working with the public. So the best way to recognize everyone's birthday is via email.

The Internet has thousands of free or low cost e-cards you can send. I personally love Blue Mountain's online assortment of talking, singing, and dancing cards for many occasions. They even have reminders of special days coming up to help in your planning. You can send or download certain cards for free, or obtain more advanced options for just $20 a year. JibJab is another e-card option where you can put that special someone's face right in the action, or add more co-workers' pictures to increase the fun (with their knowledge and permission of course).

I like e-cards, but being the creative person that I am, I love to use email to send my own unique message and copy my co-workers. For example, I do news releases for our organization. I recently wrote a fake news release to honor my friend Micah's birthday, complete with a big headline and quotes of praise about him from our director. Since we are an organization focused on STEM (Science, technology, engineering, and math) education concentrating on the wonders of the universe, I sprinkled the release with astronomy and outer space terms. He loved it.

Another coworker's birthday arrived just as I was coming down with the flu. I emailed her a silly poem before my brain was completely foggy. I've learned that if you go the poem route, it doesn't have to be perfect. In fact, people like it better if it's a bit flawed. Kelly, the birthday girl, wrote back that she was so thrilled to get the email that she was near tears. I was happy that I took those few minutes even when I wasn't feeling well to make her feel special for her birthday.

No time for e-cards or creativity? Even a simple message with a cartoon inserted in the email can bring someone a lot of joy. Here are some easy things you can say:

Joy to You and Me (At Work!)

1. No fuss, no muss, just a big birthday wish from all of us! This one is great for people like my coworker Kevin who truly doesn't want a lot of fuss for his birthday. In fact it took me months to figure out the right date because he wouldn't tell anyone!
2. Hear ye, hear ye, to all let it be known that today is Joe (or Jill) Schmoe's birthday!
3. Roses are red, violets are blue, just taking some time to say Happy Birthday to you.
4. Say "Happy Birthday" in another language. This is great for someone who has recently traveled to a different country or who is about to.

No matter what you do, even if your email takes just a minute, your coworker will greatly appreciate that someone took the time to recognize him or her.

Signs

Perhaps a real card just isn't an option due to time or money. Or not everyone at your company or department has email. A sign posted in a common area or on an office door or cubicle can still make someone feel special and show that you care. Once again, the Internet has you covered. Birthday banners, signs, templates, posters, flyers - you name it, you can find it online for free. In just two minutes you can locate a perfect sign, print it out, and tape it to a wall.

Or maybe you have some time and the ability to be creative. You can use some of the previous email ideas for signs as well. Remember Cora, the princess? I found a cartoon of a princess in a car waving in a parade, enlarged it, and printed it out on an 11X17 piece of paper. Guess whose face I pasted in place of the cartoon princess?

You could also simply put "Happy Birthday from the Gang," and list everyone's names underneath. Or have everyone sign it personally on a lunch hour. Throw in some clip art and you're done!

Dressing up for Halloween and Christmas

Just a short note for Halloween - unless you have religious reasons for not enjoying it, I think dressing up in an appropriate costume at work is super-awesome and fun! It makes the day seem special and happy. Just make certain it's OK with your company or organization and that others are doing the same thing. If you see customers on Halloween, you can bring them a joyful surprise with your costume. Be careful that it doesn't hamper your work in any way. Sometimes my office has been more conservative in this area, so I just add a touch of Halloween in my attire such as some fun jack o' lantern socks, spider earrings, or funky eye makeup. Grown-ups can have a blast with this holiday! It's a great time for potlucks and of course, yummy treats.

You can dress up around Christmas time if you celebrate it as well. We always put on festive attire for our Christmas party potlucks at both the Town of Field's Corner and the soil and water conservation district. This ranged from ugly Christmas sweaters to ties featuring Santa and his reindeer to sparkly sequined tops.

Dressing up for either or both holidays is a great way to build camaraderie and a sense of being a team.

No matter what you choose - wearing something different, passing around a card, creating an unusual email, or putting together a sign - it all takes just minutes to do but can have a huge impact on your team or for the recipient. Do you have a little more time or cash? Read on for some bigger things you can do for these special occasions!

Amy Thornton

"Oh, that's bold. I like bold!" *Greg McCauley, Link Institute Director*

Chapter Seven

Going Above and Beyond

Birthday cake. Birthday pie. Birthday cookies. Most of the time you can't go wrong with a yummy birthday dessert. Even people who have special dietary needs can have desserts with all of the gluten and sugar-free options available now. Or if you have someone who is eating extremely healthy, you can be quite creative with fruit. I've seen a watermelon "cake" online made with 100% fruit that looks absolutely heavenly!

Whether you buy it, bake it, or make it, a birthday dessert can mean a lot to a coworker and bring everyone together for a few minutes of happiness. My father-in-law, Ryan, made it a point to remember everyone's birthday and to bring in a cake. One 18-year-old girl who had a difficult family life burst into tears when he brought her one for her special day.

"No one has ever done this for me before," she cried.

I was touched at the soil and water conservation district when my boss asked what my favorite cake was. I told her I liked German chocolate cake and was blown away the next day when she brought in a homemade one for my birthday! This is one busy lady, so having her take that time meant a lot to me. My friend Clarissa is a donut fanatic, so of course we had to have a donut cake for her special day.

Which brings me to my next point. Sometimes it's just not possible to break away during the day to cut a cake or other dessert. When times got busy at the Town of Field's Corner and it was difficult to coordinate schedules, we often gathered for a birthday breakfast before the official start of the workday. Sometimes it was healthy, sometimes it wasn't (French toast casserole anyone?), but enjoying a treat together was a wonderful way to start the birthday person's day.

If you plan a bit ahead, you can take it to the next level and have potluck lunches for birthdays or holidays. One large department at the Town of Field's Corner held a potluck each month to honor everyone's birthday for that month. They held it on a specific day each time so staff members knew to keep their calendars clear.

To prevent everyone from bringing all desserts or all side dishes, creating a sign-up sheet template comes in handy once again. Start off with a main dish section, followed by side dishes, desserts, and drinks (non-alcoholic of course!) Print it out when needed and post it in a common area along with a pen so it's easy for people to sign up to bring a dish. I always post the sign-up sheet at least a week ahead of time so people can think of what they need for their grocery lists.

My father-in-law always had potluck lunches, and this is one of the reasons people wanted to be on his crew!

I always enjoyed special Christmas potluck lunches when I worked for local governments. Sometimes we played easy games like Uno or did Secret Santa reveals. "White elephant gift" lunches were also a blast, especially when you could steal a gift up to three different times.

It might be tough to find an entire hour for a potluck lunch, so this is another opportunity to go with breakfast instead. If you make this big enough, no one will need to eat lunch later on! And sometimes a breakfast can involve easier dishes than a lunch, which might help time-crunched coworkers.

Joy to You and Me (At Work!)

If you need to make things even simpler, collecting a few dollars from people and ordering pizzas is sometimes the way to go and can really boost morale! Taking 15 minutes to laugh over a couple slices of pepperoni can help a team through a challenging project.

And remember to celebrate co-workers' big achievements as well as birthdays. Running a half or full marathon, having a first child, celebrating the opening night of the play that an employee is starring in - these are all huge accomplishments that deserve a show of support from coworkers. I've made signs that everyone has written good luck messages on for people running marathons. I've also participated in some wonderful birthday lunch showers thrown over the weekend for those that are about to have their first baby. And I was so touched when my coworkers decorated my cubicle years ago to wish me luck for the opening night of a local play I starred in.

So we've done quite a bit of talking about food, which is probably making you just as hungry as I am. Sometimes people's diets are so challenging that food isn't even an option. Or maybe you want to add some more fun to those yummy celebrations.

Can you sing? This is probably one of the more "out there" ideas in this book, but sometimes I'll make up a song for someone. Most of the time it's to the tune of a popular song. For example, I went all "Weird Al" on my coworker Jenny and turned the popular Aerosmith song "Janie's Got a Gun" into "Jenny's Got a Bun". She often styled her pretty long blonde hair into a striking, professional looking bun. Jenny loved it!

You can sing to someone individually, or if you're brave and/or crazy like me, you can sing to them when everyone is gathered together. I'm talking about going beyond the typical

"Happy Birthday to You" song, people. This is where you can be bold! Just make certain the person won't be embarrassed by all the attention. And don't worry if your singing isn't perfect. Come on, look at the popularity of all those karaoke places!

I also like to sing a special song to someone on their voicemail. This is particularly great when they are away on a business trip and not around for their actual birthday. Or when I'm not in the office for some reason. Or when I just want to sing to someone and not have everyone in the world hear it. The advantage to a voicemail song is they can keep it as long as they like and play it back when they need to be cheered up in the future.

Remember my silly email poems? You could also recite a fun poem to someone during a gathering over food, one on one, or on voicemail. The weirder the better. And don't fret about perfection here. Your sixth grade English teacher isn't going to come around and slap you for rhymes that don't quite work or the incorrect iambic pentameter. You don't even have to make up a poem. Just hop online. The Poetry Foundation has over 40,000 poems you can choose from. PoemHunter.com has poetry from all over the world. And NetPoets.com enables you to search for poems by keyword. Their poetry map helps you find different types of poems, and the Poetry Buffet category has humorous, holiday, and special occasion poems.

Maybe singing and poetry are well beyond your comfort zone. How about decorating someone's workspace for a special occasion? This can take as little as five minutes or as long as 45. For this category, I rely once again on the dollar store. You can get streamers, balloons, and other fun doodads at a reasonable cost. I like to stock up once a year so I always have decorations on hand.

This is another area where you have to proceed with caution. Most people will love coming in to work to see their special day recognized with decorations. If you know the person well and are certain they'll love all kinds of crazy decorations, go for it. If not, it's best to be on the safe side and go with some simple balloons and streamers. No matter what, make certain your decorations don't hamper their work efforts. You don't want the birthday guy or gal spending a half hour undoing your efforts just so they could get to their desk when they're approaching a big deadline.

And, make certain nothing gets broken in their office or workspace. I learned this lesson the hard way. I did some elaborate decorations for Boss's Day years ago. While disassembling my creation, my boss broke one of her knickknacks that she had gotten at a farmers market. I felt terrible and did my best to replace it, but it was a unique item and I couldn't truly come close.

Sometimes you don't have to spend a dime to perfectly decorate someone's office, cubicle, or locker. I redeemed myself years later from the Boss's Day debacle by putting small rocks from my rock wall at home on a different boss's desk. Gail was a self-proclaimed "rock hound," an amateur geologist. When I realized I would be out of the office on Boss's Day due to a vacation, I stayed a few minutes late one Friday. Since Boss's Day was the following Monday, I placed various rocks around her desk along with a table tent sign that simply said, "You ROCK as our boss!" I smiled when I got her voicemail of appreciation on my cell phone while strolling through Epcot with my family that Monday!

At this point you may be thinking, "There is absolutely no way I can do even half of these things. I don't have the time. Or the nerve. Or the creativity." That's OK. I want to challenge you to try at least a few of these ideas, some of which take only a couple minutes and don't require courage. The idea of bringing joy to the workplace is to increase productivity and reduce stress. We don't want to make it more difficult to get our work done.

As I mentioned earlier, I like to stock up once a year on decorations and cards. This drastically reduces your preparation time for some of these ideas. Maybe during some down time you can find a couple of clever poems online and save them for certain coworkers. One fun thing that people have done for me is to look up highlights from the exact day I was born. MyBirthdayFacts.com will share fun facts about your birthday and famous events. It also shows what famous people share your special day. Simply select the exact date and you instantly have your information. My friends taped some fun facts to my door for my birthday years ago and I got a kick out of them - plus, we all shared a laugh. Just make certain someone is not sensitive about their age on this one.

While we are on that subject, watch out for the rare person who gets depressed on their birthday. Bringing in black balloons and adult diapers might make most people laugh when they turn 50, but some people won't appreciate the humor and might get upset. If someone is dreading a birthday, keep things simple and low-key with a card, if anything.

Joy to You and Me (At Work!)

You still may think you won't have time to try out these suggestions. Start out with one or two and see what happens. You might get hooked on bringing joy to others like I am and discover that you have more time than you think! You'll find it's well worth it to show everyone how much you care about them.

Before we move on to the next chapter, let's talk about what truly gigantic, humongous, beyond the ordinary things you can do to bring joy to the workplace if you own a company or are in upper management. Let's look at some examples from our friends at Salesforce.

Salesforce CEO Marc Benioff adopted the Hawaiian belief of Ohana when he created his company in 1999. If you've never seen the Disney movie Lilo and Stitch, you may not be familiar with this concept. Ohana focuses on all components of a family being intertwined and bound with one another. And this Salesforce culture extends to *everyone,* from interns all the way up to Mr. Benioff himself.

Ohana represents the idea that family members, i.e. Salesforce employees, are responsible for one another. This belief also extends to their partners, customers, and communities.

"We collaborate, take care of one another, have fun together, and work to leave the world a better place," writes Jody Kohner, Senior Vice President of the Employee Marketing & Engagement team who blogged about the concept in February 2017 on the company's website.[30]

Intern Rob Desisto blogged later in 2017 saying that Ohana is the real deal.[31]

"I was treated on day one like someone who mattered and was valued by the company and organization," he writes.

"People were just as invested in the success of my projects as they were in their own personal projects, which was something that I was not expecting right out of the gate."

Everything that happens in the company is made with Ohana in mind.

"I'm with a community that cares for both my wellbeing and my success, and enables me to be a better person as I continue my journey from college student to full-time worker," he continues.

When touring the Indianapolis office, you can literally see how much the company cares for its employees. Corner offices are gone and everyone has a view. Employees can grab a snack and meet in a lounge space. Green carpet represents grass and brown hardwood floors represent gravel walkways. A meditation room is available for those who need to take a break and de-stress.

ArcelorMittal, a multinational steel manufacturing corporation, also treats their employees to some joyful experiences. My best friend works at the Burns Harbor, Indiana location. I've loved hearing her stories about their quarterly crossword puzzle challenges, Easter Egg Hunts, and department softball games. On Health and Safety Day, employees receive chair massages and paraffin wax treatments. Every Friday is jeans day in her department. My friend has enjoyed team-building days where she goes to the beach with her department. She gets to leave early on occasion on Fridays. Pizza, donuts, and ice cream socials round out the fun.

Smaller companies can implement similar ideas. When I was hired to work for a meeting planning company in 1997, I knew from the start that the owners, Ned and Mindy, would care a great deal about their employees. In fact I was their first one! As the company grew, they rewarded us with team-building time such as an evening with dinner and seeing a jaw-dropping Cirque du Soleil show. They hosted a free self-defense class one afternoon for us with concepts that I can still remember 20+ years later.

When we moved offices and had a spare closet, Ned and Mindy turned it into a "nap room," complete with a cozy black recliner. I spent the occasional lunch hour in that room and can't begin to describe the boost to my energy during the afternoons that followed! I loved working there and only left because I knew I was ready to start a family and didn't want to travel anymore. I've visited the company since then and I can tell how happy the employees are. Some of them have been there for a couple of decades now! The company is thriving, growing, and successful, and I'm certain it's because of the way they treat their employees.

The Town of Field's Corner does an employee appreciation week every year thanks to generous local sponsors. This usually involves an ice cream social, chair massages, and an employee picnic to end the week. The human resources department spends many hours to make all of this happen and I know it's still deeply appreciated to this day.

There are hundreds more stories of how companies both big and small are going above and beyond to bring joy to both their employees and customers. I'll share more customer stories later. What I want to stress is that if you are the head of a company or one of its leaders, I encourage you to learn about the unique ways you can show employees how much you care.

Amy Thornton

They don't always have to involve a lot of money or effort, but can give you the kind of success you never imagine.

Joy to You and Me (At Work!)

"So long, farewell, auf Wiedersehen, adieu" *The Sound of Music*

Chapter Eight

Welcome... Farewell... And (Appropriate) Pranks

It's especially important to bring joy to the new kids on the block at our companies. Helping to start them off on the right foot makes them feel confident and happy about working there and prevents turnover. High rates of turnover are bad news for companies. In an article from March 2013, Inc.com gives five reasons for this:[32]

1. Talent shortages are real in some industries.
2. If time is short now for training, what will it look like in the future with high turnover?
3. A bad economy means only the best find jobs.
4. Unhappy employees don't perform as well.
5. The best way to find good candidates is networking with existing staff. If your current staff members aren't happy, they're certainly not going to refer good people to the company.

Whether you're in upper or middle management, mid or entry level, you can bring joy to help set the stage for new employees to start well, stick around, and work with the company longer.

Obviously you most likely won't know the new person, so now is not the time to do any "over the top" stuff. I traditionally like to invite a new employee to breakfast or lunch if she is a female. It's also fun to work with your department to host a potluck for the person's first day. I always create a welcome sign and have it waiting on his or her door or entrance. Some people have kept their sign for months! If your company or department does have a party fund, a small bouquet of flowers or balloons is a nice touch as well.

What about when someone is leaving a company for either a better opportunity or retirement? Here's where it is vital to be joyful whether you are the person leaving or someone else is.

If You Are Leaving

If I had to pick one of the top three takeaways I want you to get from this book, this would be one of them: Always leave a job gracefully. Never burn a bridge. Never. Ever.

You may be really mad and want to storm out the door and quit instantly. You may think this is the absolute worst place to work since the dawn of time. But unless someone has truly wronged you or broken the law, write the kindest letter of resignation possible and give your two weeks notice. And keep a positive attitude every minute of every day of those two weeks.

Why do I feel so strongly about this? I'll share an example from my own life.

You've heard me mention the Town of Field's Corner a time or two - or 10. I worked there for nine years and as I mentioned before, I enjoyed most every day I was there. I started out as an administrative assistant in their economic development department and was promoted to Grant Coordinator after six months thanks to my strong grant professional experience. A couple of years later I went on to create and lead the city's Sustain Field's Corner committee. Both endeavors led to millions of dollars for the town and some great team efforts to help it be more sustainable.

After seven years, however, I started to wonder if I were really doing what I was meant to do in life. I think God heard my doubts because a couple months later I was told that my position was changing and that I would become a community engagement coordinator. I was moved to the "closet office" that I referred to earlier in this book, but tried to make the best of things. Unfortunately, my new boss was the one who didn't care for my cheerful personality. I was also stuck in lots of meetings, and I am not a fan of meetings. I get "antsy" quickly. I started to plan and lead more events. I am not an event person - I love to help with them, but being in charge of them gives me tremendous stress.

But I wouldn't have written this book if I weren't the type of person to see the bright side in life. I began to take on more volunteer coordinator activities in this role and I loved that part of the job. My grant and Sustain Field's Corner duties were waning, which made me sad, but I was determined to make the best of things.

In the fall of 2015, my boss left for another opportunity. I was excited and thought I would finally be truly happy in my job. Imagine my shock when I was told the day before Veterans Day that I was being placed back into the administrative assistant position for the economic development department - the same position I had started in nine years earlier. My pay was also being cut.

No one asked me how I felt about this nor was I ever given a reason for the dramatic change. Everyone had always praised my efforts and my attitude so these actions made no sense to me. I was devastated. I spent one evening sobbing on the couch in my husband's arms, sad to see my efforts taken away after nine years.

I couldn't possibly stay, but was blessed to find the job at the county's soil and water conservation district along with a part-time grant consulting position. I wrote a nice letter of resignation and gave my two-week notice when everyone returned from the holidays in January of 2016. I had realized that God was answering my silent prayer from early 2014. It wasn't quite the way I imagined, but it made me stronger. I worked hard to wrap up as much as I could over the next two weeks to make it easier for the people who would be taking over my tasks. I also let them know they could get in touch with me with any questions later on.

And then, I went shopping - but not for myself. I wanted to give everyone in my department a small memento to thank them for being not just my coworkers, but my friends as well. I thoroughly enjoyed getting everyone's presents and seeing the looks on their faces when they opened them on my final day. They in turn threw a wonderful breakfast celebration for me that included yummy treats and various pictures from my time with the town. I stayed until the very last minute on that day double-checking everything.

In the months and years that followed, I never talked badly about my former coworkers. In fact, in December 2016, I actually thanked the town manager after a public meeting for what happened, letting him know it was the push I needed to find something better for myself!

Fast forward to 2017 and it's time for my family to demolish our detached garage and build a new one. Guess what entities I

Joy to You and Me (At Work!)

had to work with quite a bit for this project? Multiple town departments. And every single person was kind and helpful during each step along the way. This project is still in progress, but I know I can reach out to a town employee and be treated well. If I had left with a bad attitude and burned a bridge, I know this process would not have gone so pleasantly. I don't think anyone would have intentionally caused my family or me harm, but I doubt that they would have gone above and beyond for me like they have been doing.

And when my current organization, the Link Observatory Space Science Institute, wanted to talk to different leaders in my county about building their future space center, the Field's Corner town manager department scheduled a meeting for us rather quickly. It was wonderful to meet with some of my former coworkers knowing that we all still had a good relationship.

In addition to these examples, you always want to leave a job gracefully because you never know when you may need a reference for a future opportunity. Have you ever heard of the six degrees of separation? This is the theory that we are only six or fewer people away from knowing everyone in the entire world. I believe this theory. Have you ever had a conversation with someone and been blown away that they know a family member or friend of yours? Companies and organizations talk to one another, and with our technology today, they don't even have to be in the same state or country. Why give a past employer a chance to say something negative about you?

So remember, always give your notice, don't burn bridges, and be joyful until the very end. You never know what the future may hold and you'll feel at peace with how you left things.

If Someone Else Is Leaving

If someone is retiring or moving on to work for a different company or organization, this is a golden opportunity to show them appreciation for all of their (hopefully) good work. Remember, we spend a lot of waking hours with our coworkers, and they are often like a second family. Saying farewell to them should be a joyful, positive experience that they'll always remember.

As a rule of thumb, what you do for someone who's been with the company for a couple of years should probably be different than what you do for someone who's retiring after 20 years. I thought the breakfast open house that the Town of Field's Corner had for me was just perfect for my amount of time there. It was a simple two-hour celebration that enabled my fellow employees and members of the community to stop by to chat with me. I often look back fondly on photos from that morning.

When our summer intern, Kenny, left to go back to school from the soil and water conservation district in August of 2016, we all knew we wanted to do something special for him. Even though he had only been there four months, he had worked hard for us and implemented some great new ideas. Kenny was positive, fun, and always went above and beyond in his duties. He wasn't the typical intern due to the fact that he was older, in his late-20s, had already served eight years in the Air Force, and was now working to finish college and get his bachelor's degree.

I wrote a poem for him that was funny and filled with inside jokes. I ended it thanking him for all he had done for us and posted the poem on his computer so he would see it first thing on the morning of his last day. He was absolutely blown away - and we hadn't even treated him to lunch yet!

"I didn't get anything like this even when I left my base," Kenny said. He was genuinely touched that we were giving him such a warm farewell. We went on to enjoy one of the best barbecue lunches that I've ever had! I'll never forget the look on his face and his sincere appreciation.

Of course, celebrations for someone who is retiring after many years can go up to an entirely different level. I think open houses with appetizers, drinks, cards, and gifts are wonderful. You should always talk to the person first to see what their comfort level is in this instance.

If you need gift ideas, US News and World Report shared 10 classic and unique retirement gifts in a May 2017 article.[33] These include:

1. Objects noting years of service such as a plaque, watch, or necklace.
2. Hobby and travel gifts. Any gifts relating to the person's hobby or to travel such as a suitcase, beautiful luggage tag, or durable toiletry bag can be very meaningful.
3. Experiences such as tickets to a sporting event or a gift certificate to a favorite restaurant. This is great for someone who loves a certain sport or enjoys going out to eat.
4. Industry gifts representing what the retiree created, bought, or sold during his or her employment. For example, when my first boss from the soil and water conservation district retired, we all chipped in and had a local artist paint a clay soil tile for him. Clay soil tiles were used by farmers for years to help with underground drainage. Our boss, Jim, helped people use these properly during his 30 years with the

district. The artist painted different things Jim enjoyed doing in life such as bicycling. It took him a second to figure out what the gift was, but once he did his face broke out into a wide grin!

5. Humorous gifts. Once again, be careful here. If the person has been fun loving and enjoyed doing humorous things for others, you're probably safe here. Ask around if you're not certain.

6. Group projects such as a photo with a mat surrounding it that everyone can sign.

7. Contributions to his or her favorite charity.

8. Social invitations for future get-togethers. This is especially important because the person is most likely leaving not just coworkers, but dear friends.

9. Sentimental gifts like photo albums, scrapbooks, collections of thank you notes from customers, etc. These gifts can take a lot of time and effort, so if you know someone is retiring in a couple of months, start early and delegate different components to various people. These gifts are incredibly meaningful to both the retiree and his or her family.

Whether someone has been at a company for a couple of months, a few years, or a couple of decades, helping then leave on a positive note (if the circumstances for them leaving were good) is a kind gesture. It's a smart one, too. I think most companies and organizations would agree that they want their former employees to speak well of them. And it doesn't hurt to have another voice out there helping to recruit talented workers.

Pranks

Pranks in the workplace are another way to bring a lot of joy. They can be absolutely hilarious and remembered with laughter for years to come (do you recall Jim and Pam from the television show *The Office?*). However, without being careful, just the opposite can happen. You don't want to get fired; written up; delay important work; harass someone; waste, damage, or steal office supplies or equipment; or cause any injuries! This is another instance to remember to always be sensitive to others and when in doubt, talk to Human Resources.

Make certain you know the person well before pulling your prank. One of my bosses enjoyed collecting Cubebots, which are small, posable wooden robots. I added to his collection by buying a couple for Boss's Day and his birthday. He liked to keep them on the front of his desk. Once a week or so when he was away from the department, I would sneak into his office and let the Cubebots go on "adventures"! Sometimes they would have workouts, play leapfrog, hold their own meetings, and go on creative excursions. Everyone got a kick out of this and looked forward to seeing what the Cubebots would do next. Unfortunately, this is the same boss who did not like my personality, so he finally told me the adventures had to stop. Some people simply don't have a sense of humor and don't like positive people. Oh well, bummer for them.

I also goofed for my friend Matt's birthday at the soil and water office. I taped a funny sign to his door early on the morning of the big day and hid in a nearby closet to see his reaction. Unfortunately, what I witnessed was shock (after laughing at the sign) upon realizing he didn't have a key to unlock his office – and when I had shut the door, it locked automatically! We had to call someone from the county's maintenance department, who ended up crawling through the ceiling to unlock the door because no one had a key. I was mortified to say the least, and poor Matt lost 45 minutes of his workday.

Now that I've tossed you the disclaimers, let's get to the fun! Pranks can vary from the simple to the extreme. I'll never forget walking into the women's restroom one day at the soil and water conservation district and finding some fake poo in the corner! After I jumped nearly two feet high, I laughed practically all afternoon about it. Of course I had to find the culprit, who was none other than the aforementioned Matt. Matt is one of those guys who appears to be completely innocent on the outside but is quite devious on the inside. Apparently the fake poo was actually used in one of the district's displays a couple of years previously! So Matt didn't even spend a dime for it.

Naturally I put it away in my drawer where no one could find it and somehow it reappeared in the men's restroom a couple of months later - when Matt was the only guy in the office one morning. It was rather gratifying to hear his gasp of surprise and laughter that day. Remember, it's all about good timing and plotting, folks!

During a winter staff meeting a few weeks later, our boss asked who had built a mini snowman on the hood of her truck. Matt happened to be away at a "consultation" at the time. We all quickly figured out who Frosty's creator was.

The Queen of all Pranksters in my opinion was my friend, Cora, the princess. Beneath that professional, polished, public relations exterior was a truly diabolical mind.

Joy to You and Me (At Work!)

Our Human Resources Director, Hillary, and one of our awesome maintenance employees, Ted, always parked in the same spots next to each other since they were the first two people in the building every morning. Ted went to lunch <u>at 11 a.m.</u> and Hillary usually went <u>at 11:30.</u> Cora went outside one day after Hillary had left for lunch and put up cones and tape around their parking spots along with signs saying, "Parking reserved - Violators' vehicles will be towed and sold for scrap metal".

"The other time I waited until after they had both left for lunch (since my office overlooked the parking lot, I could just look out to make sure they had already left) and went out and parked my car diagonally so that I was taking up both of their parking spots," Cora shared with me.

Another theme you can use in pranking people is a college rivalry. In my home state of Indiana, there's no better rivalry than Purdue and Indiana University. Both Cora and I attended IU - naturally, the best school. Our friend Josie, however, is a proud graduate of Purdue. All three of us worked in the same suite for years, which gave us many opportunities for fun.

"I played IU pranks on Josie's car, but she never knew it until I confessed when I left," Cora said. "She always thought it was someone else and never had known it was me! One time I found a big magnetic IU sticker for cars on clearance for $1 and bought it and put it on the back of her car. Then I watched with delight out my window one afternoon when she drove out of the parking lot, not knowing she was driving a vehicle with a big IU magnet on the back."

"There was one time I put one of those flags that are secured by a car's window on the passenger side of her car, but I don't remember if she drove off not knowing it was there or if she saw it and took it off before she left," Cora continued.

Another time Cora found a framed IU poster at a garage sale for $1 and secretly replaced a picture in Josie's office with the IU one.

Before you feel too sorry for Josie, all of us traded "gifts" throughout the years, and somehow I ended up with a drawer full of Purdue paraphernalia. A dear friend of the family who happened to love that school in West Lafayette, Indiana was glad to take the items off my hands.

Cora's crowning achievement, pun intended, was her final prank for Ted when she left the Town of Field's Corner. Remember my story about fake poo in the bathroom? Let's just say Cora took that to a whole new level for Ted. Despite her not taking the "leaving a job gracefully" path for this individual, she knew Ted would love the joke. Cora and Ted are still friends who talk and get together regularly. That fake poo story is probably still circulating around Town Hall to this day!

If you've never done pranks before, and are willing to give them a try to bring smiles and laughter to the workplace, there's no better day to start than April Fools' Day. I decided to use the holiday as an excuse to pound on the bathroom door and startle Josie as she was washing her hands a few years ago. She was suddenly quite alert for the rest of the day! It's good to help our fellow employees be more energetic, right?

I could go on and on with various examples of pranks for the workplace, but you can look up several for yourself on Pinterest or Google. You can search for ones specifically for April Fools' Day if you like. Some pranks are easy, some involve low-tech computer maneuvers, and some are the products of true geniuses. You can also watch The Office for some brilliant ideas!

To build your courage, keep in mind - office pranks are everywhere. I've read that Microsoft employees and Facebook founder Mark Zuckerberg aren't even immune from them!

If you're still nervous about pranks, simply Google "harmless" or "discreet" workplace pranks for some hilarious, but safe ideas. I've also found some when I typed in "pranks that won't get you fired." And remember to never cross into mean, harassing, or nasty territory. In fact, whenever I plan any prank, I want the victim - oops, I mean recipient - to love it and laugh harder than anyone else. This is all about bringing joy to the workplace, not anger or sadness. Keep that in mind and soon you will be the master prankster at work!

Amy Thornton

"We all need somebody to lean on." *Bill Withers*

Chapter Nine

Comfort and Joy

Up until now we've been pretty light-hearted in this book. But we all know that life isn't always sunshine and roses. In fact, it's often filled with tragedies and heartache. Switching from bringing joy to bringing calm and comfort is obviously appropriate for these situations.

Unfortunately the worst things in life don't always occur outside of work hours. Sadly, I know what I'm talking about. One morning during my first real full-time job as an advertising sales director for a small local newspaper, I got a terrible phone call from my sister, Vicky. She called to let me know that my dad had suffered a massive heart attack while on vacation with my mother and their friends in Florida. I remember sinking to my knees in front of my desk. And I was back on my knees 45 minutes later when Vicky called to let me know he had passed away.

I'll never forget what a comfort my boss Patty was that morning. We had a small office and she was the only other person there at that moment. Patty was at my side with tissues, water, prayers, and a strong hug. As I sat there in shock waiting for my husband to pick me up from work, she held my hand and gave me a legal pad and pen. Patty helped me keep breathing and guided me to write down a list of things that would need to be done before I left for my hometown in northern Indiana to be with family and friends. I can still hear her gentle voice to this day.

Hopefully we'll never encounter situations like these, but it's important to be prepared for them nonetheless. Whether it's receiving life-shattering news or experiencing some sort of trauma on the job like a major injury, we should think through what to do when the worst happens.

Bigger companies may have a human resources person or department for these situations. But even in that case, we should still be prepared. You never know when that person or members of that department may be away for some reason.

Make certain that emergency numbers are posted in a common area where everyone can get to them quickly. Obviously 911 should be at the top of the list. Other important numbers include the local hospital, emergency room, urgent care center, police department, fire department, and poison control center.

If someone receives unthinkable news like what I shared earlier, it's important to delegate responsibilities calmly and quickly. Having someone drive a coworker home, to the hospital, or wherever he or she needs to go should be at the top of the list if a family member can't get there. No one should be behind the wheel in these situations.

To Patty's credit, I believe what she did for me was perfect. She let me know right away to take as much time as I needed. Patty was by my side every minute up until my husband arrived. Having her help to create a much-needed plan kept me going and prevented me from falling completely apart.

What sorts of things can we do to bring comfort after the tragedy or bad news has eased up? This is definitely a delicate area. Obviously sending flowers or making a donation to charity for a funeral, for instance, is appropriate. Showing your support by attending a viewing if it is in town is meaningful as well.

When my father-in-law Ryan returned to work after his son, my husband's brother Ralph, was killed in an automobile accident in 1999, he posted a simple sign outside his door. It let everyone know he appreciated their concern, but that he needed to focus while at work and wasn't able to talk about the situation yet. Of course, most people won't spell everything out as clearly as this.

When I returned to work a week after my dad's funeral, I was counting on having the distraction of my job to get me on the path to healing. I knew that keeping busy would help me turn around eventually. I can't recall what my coworkers did at this point, as it is somewhat of a blur. I think what most people would appreciate in this situation is hearing something like, "We're always here for you and want to respect your wishes during this difficult time. If there is anything you need, just let us know."

Little, quiet, comforting touches can mean so much to a coworker in a trying time. Taking turns providing meals to someone is a weight off their shoulders when their life has gone haywire. Online sites such as Meal Train, Take Them a Meal, Food Tidings, and others make it easy for everyone to sign up for specific days and times to deliver meals for coworkers who are experiencing illness or other challenges. On a lighter note, they're also great for when someone has a new baby! I like to make something that's easy for people to freeze in case they have bunches of food given to them. They can always enjoy a meal at a later time when needed.

I love to share a couple bags of my favorite tea with coworkers when I know they're feeling down. As people have known for centuries, there's something soothing and comforting about a hot cup of tea. Or coffee, cocoa, or whatever people prefer. In the spring I like to pick bouquets of lily of the valley from my front yard and surprise my female coworkers with them. These little bell shaped flowers can fill an entire room with their soft fragrance. I even pick some for myself to brighten my mood during rainy spring days.

A little card with a special note to let someone know you're thinking of them can also mean the world during challenging times. One of my favorite gift shops has beautiful $.99 blank cards that I stock up on from time to time just for these situations.

And who hasn't experienced starting to feel ill at work? Coming to the aid of a coworker who's not feeling well can mean the world to them. Offering to get him or her some aspirin or another pain reliever along with some tea can make a big difference. My father-in-law, Ryan, once came to the rescue of a male employee when he was throwing up in the bathroom! Ryan placed wet paper towels on the back of his neck to help the nausea pass. It amazed his employee to have Ryan offering this comfort at such a difficult time.

On a less of a big bummer note, my wonderful, joyful friend Dan Walsh used to have his students write a "golden gem" every afternoon in their assignment notebook to brighten their day. They were to write down something positive that happened before they left for the day. Dan followed suit and did the same exercise in his own notebook. His students would write things like "I made someone laugh" or "I got a compliment today."

Joy to You and Me (At Work!)

One day a boy named Mike asked if he could write down two! Dan told him, "Of course."

This activity had a ripple effect. Mike's mother, Christy, was a principal. She later told Dan during a parent-teacher conference that she was having her teachers do the same thing!

Thinking through what we can do to help someone at work who may be down or experiencing heartache is wise. But what happens when a tragedy occurs in the community surrounding your workplace? This is where coworkers can come together and practically move mountains.

In 2007 a bright young man in our community named Michael Treinen was diagnosed with Acute Myleoid Leukemia three weeks before his high school graduation. He went into remission the following December, but the cancer quickly returned in January of 2008. Michael began receiving treatment at Riley Children's Hospital in Indianapolis and at the end of March of that year his next step was a bone marrow transplant. Michael needed to have the transplant quickly in order to survive. After some research, his parents knew the best place for his treatment was Children's Hospital in Seattle, Washington.

Unfortunately, the Treinens needed to earn $500,000 in four days to secure a bone marrow transplant for Michael, whose medical bills had exceeded his insurance policy's lifetime benefit limit. His mother Kelly started a heartfelt email chain on a Sunday asking people to pray, send a donation of at least $20 to a special fund at a local bank, and pass the email along to at least 20 other people. Amazingly, the e-mail chain worked. Countless people from inside and outside Hamilton County -

and beyond - quickly began to donate. Soon the news spread around the entire state of Indiana, the nation, and the world.

And the Town of Field's Corner employees rallied together as well. I remember feeling this amazing sense of togetherness and spirit as we all emailed, phoned, and talked to various departments in person. And of course we spread the word to as many people as possible outside of our municipality. We all were on edge practically every hour that week waiting for updates on the total amount raised. Many of us prayed together for Michael and his family, which was thankfully OK in our workplace.

By Thursday afternoon, the Treinens had raised well over $700,000. I'll never forget the chills that traveled through me when we all got the news in my department. And another miracle happened - the family was notified that Michael qualified for a state insurance program that covered 60% of the cost of his transplant. The money in the fund helped pay for the transplant and the cost of Michael's recovery. What was left went to help other children battling cancer.

I wish I could say everything turned out fine. Sadly, the cancer still won and Michael passed away in May 2008.

His family went on to form the Michael Treinen Foundation to assist and enhance the lives of individuals and their families battling Acute Myleoid Leukemia and other forms of cancer. Noblesville has an annual turkey trot 5k run/walk and 3k family walk every Thanksgiving now to raise money for this foundation - and the event is growing in popularity year after year.

We had a display of Michael's lacrosse jersey in the Town Hall lobby for years. His courage, the strength and goodness of his family, and the way our employees and an entire community rallied together to help this young man will forever be in my heart.

Bringing each other comfort in the workplace and employees coming together to help their communities are some of the most incredible ways to spread joy - a calm, quiet, soothing, yet powerful type of joy that is remembered for decades.

Amy Thornton

"Give the world the best you've got anyway." *Mother Teresa*

Chapter Ten

Some People Just Won't Get It and That's Okay

Up until now I've shared stories, research, examples, ideas, and experiences with the idea that we work with *mostly*, um, semi-normal, even-keeled, fairly pleasant individuals. People who aren't incredibly negative or down all the time. Coworkers and bosses who will probably appreciate our efforts to be joyful people spreading positivity to others - at least a little appreciative, if not more.

But even joyful, enthusiastic little me knows this is not reality. I've known it since I was a 19-year-old summer intern at a large newspaper near my hometown. I remember working in the display advertising department that year and enjoying almost every minute. Except for when I encountered the receptionist, which thankfully wasn't very often. No matter how many times I smiled at her, asked her how she was doing, or did any little positive thing, she was always Little Miss Grumpy Pants, to put it as nicely as possible.

Being young, this bothered me. My friend and neighbor, Adele, who worked with me, could tell that I was troubled. She finally pulled me aside and explained to me that not everyone likes a cheerful person.

"And that's OK," Adele said. "Don't ever change - and just avoid her as much as you can. You're going back to school in August anyway!"

No matter where you work, there's usually at least one person who rocks the boat, creates some challenges, and is negative overall. It can be our boss, manager, administrative assistant, fellow assembly line worker, and yes, even a receptionist (and aren't they supposed to be - most of the time - friendly?). These people can make it difficult to accomplish our normal tasks at work, let alone allow us to spread joy.

Then there is the type of person I'll describe as The Wall. This person sees work as *work* and nothing else. No fun is ever allowed, and God forbid your personal life or any discussion of it enters the department. The Wall often hates his or her job and absolutely nothing is going to change that feeling. The Wall is there each day to work eight or more hours and then get the hell out as quickly as humanly possible.

Bringing joy to any of these types of people is something we can't even fathom when we're struggling to just get along with them in the first place. I'd love to tell you the many ways to make life better with these individuals, but that would be an entire separate book. I can, however, share my favorite tips to help you get on the path to dealing with difficult coworkers.

I got on this path the moment I opened up Dale Carnegie's *How to Win Friends and Influence People.* As I've mentioned, it literally changed my life. Once I took and then taught the course based on this book, my skills improved. I'm definitely not an expert at dealing with difficult people, but I don't let them get to me as often and I have better relationships with them now. Not perfect relationships, but better.

One example is my tumultuous relationship with a lady I'll call Vanessa. This woman had been in her position for decades and seemed to delight in causing trouble for absolutely everyone in the company. She rarely smiled. And if you made a mistake that affected her in any way, Lord have mercy on your soul.

I made one of these mistakes. And thanks to Vanessa I paid for it over... and over... and over again. I went through anger, sadness, then anger again. I lost a lot of sleep.

One day I gave some serious thought to the principles I had learned in the Dale Carnegie course. I realized that even though I corrected my error and everything was fine with the overall project, the mistake had probably made Vanessa look perhaps a little bad to her superiors. I swallowed my pride, took out one of my $.99 blank cards, and wrote her a heartfelt note of apology. I let her know how much everyone appreciated her work and that I didn't mean to cause her any harm. I told her I would do all I could to make things up to her. I left the card on her desk along with some of my favorite chocolates.

Was everything all hunky-dory after that? No, but she was not *quite* as harsh to me. I ran into her years later after we had both moved on - me to a different company and her to retirement. Vanessa smiled and we chatted and had a delightful conversation. I sincerely hope she's doing well now.

If you need more immediate help and don't have time to take a course or read another book, I can offer you some simple things you can try right away. We've often heard that we can't control other people, - we can only control ourselves. In fact, I've honestly turned to the first part of the Serenity Prayer by Reinhold Niebuhr to help me with difficult co-workers: "God grant me the serenity to accept the things I cannot change; courage to change the things I can; and wisdom to know the difference. "

Lolly Daskal, president and CEO of Lead from Within, wrote one of the best articles I've ever seen on Inc.com on this topic in June 2015.[34] She says right in the headline that difficult coworkers can drain the joy out of our work and make us less effective. She suggests using one or more of the five A's to help deal with these individuals:

1. Accept. Daskal says this is the toughest step of all and for good reason. We have to stop wishing that the person will change and instead commit to rising above the situation. This includes not taking the bait. If we can conquer this step, we'll grow tremendously.
2. Anticipate. If we can look ahead and think about what might cause trouble with this individual, we can often avoid or mitigate it. The Boy Scout motto comes into play here – be prepared!
3. Adjust. If there are frequent misunderstandings and conflicts, take some time to examine what is happening on your side. Daskal emphasizes good listening, empathy, and openness. This can help minimize the conflicts and help you model good responses.
4. Attune. What can you appreciate about the person? In my story about Vanessa, I truly did admire her skills, which had won her numerous awards. Daskal points out that we also need to look inside ourselves for this step. We're often bothered by behaviors in others that we don't like about ourselves.
5. Avoid. This is personally my favorite solution and I'm sure it's a popular one with many folks! If possible, focus on minimizing contact with the person. Maybe another co-

worker has no trouble whatsoever with the individual and can be the occasional go-between for you. Perhaps you can use email or other technologies to communicate and get the work done. Take advantage of working from home as much as you need to if it's an option. Daskal warns us not to become a recluse or subvert other workplace relationships, however.

6. Apply. If all else fails, perhaps changing departments, transferring to a different location, or moving on to a different company altogether is the best solution. Daskal states that change can be challenging, but it also moves our careers forward.

"There will always be annoying, angry, chagrined, cross, irritating, and difficult people in our lives," Daskal summarizes. "We may not be able to fix them, but we can always care for and protect ourselves."

Perhaps just doing some small steps to improve a relationship with a difficult coworker will be victory enough for you. I hope with all my heart that you can accomplish this goal. If possible, try to bring at least a little joy to him or her once in a while. Keep things simple. Maybe you know that Crabby Joe loves this new restaurant in town and you come across a coupon for it. Keep it in your wallet or purse and when you run into him in the hallway, let them know that you saw it and you thought you'd just pass it along to him.

Perhaps Sourpuss Sally has four cats at home. When your sister downsizes and offers you a kitty cat bracelet, maybe you can casually ask if Sally would like it. Or, like what I did with

Vanessa, you can pass along some chocolate to a negative Nelly or Nelson you know has a sweet tooth.

One word of caution: don't expect anything in return from these little gestures, especially when facing The Wall! You probably won't hear a "thank you," or get one speck of appreciation. Remember that big "Accept" step mentioned earlier? You know how the person is. If you do get some appreciation, great. If not, be glad you did something anyway.

Do you remember the quote at the beginning of this chapter from Mother Teresa? It's from a series of verses that have become very popular in recent years, but there is no better advice in my opinion and I'd like to share it once again. It beautifully summarizes why we should strive to get along with our coworkers even when they are difficult and why we should be good to them. It's the perfect way for me to end this chapter:

People are often unreasonable, irrational, and self-centered.
Forgive them anyway.

If you are kind, people may accuse you of selfish, ulterior motives.
Be kind anyway.

If you are successful, you will win some unfaithful friends and some genuine enemies.
Succeed anyway.

If you are honest and sincere, people may deceive you.
Be honest and sincere anyway.

What you spend years creating, others could destroy overnight.
Create anyway.

Joy to You and Me (At Work!)

The good you do today, will often be forgotten.
Do good anyway.

Give the best you have, and it will never be enough.
Give your best anyway.

In the final analysis, it is between you and your God. It was never between you and them anyway.

Part Three

Bringing Joy to Our Customers

Amy Thornton

"Customer satisfaction is worthless. Customer loyalty is priceless." *Jeffrey Gitomer, Author, Speaker*

Chapter Eleven

Why Do We Want to Bring Joy to Our Customers When We're Doing All Kinds of Stuff Already?

Hopefully by now you're on the path to being a more joyful person/employee and you're gaining confidence about how you can spread that joy to those around you at work. Maybe you've already tried a few steps and are seeing some good results - things are more fun around the office in general and productivity is rising here and there. And perhaps you're taking some deep breaths and stepping back before exploding in front of that challenging coworker. If any of this applies to you, bravo!

Now it's time to focus on bringing joy to our customers. Whether you realize it or not, we all have customers - no matter what job we have. For example, for government workers, it's citizens. Teachers have students. Factory workers have the people who use or consume the products they help bring to fruition. You get the point.

You may be rolling your eyes at this point and thinking, "I already work hard each day to serve my clients/customers. I provide this product/service to them all the time. It's already good and meets their needs. Why do more?"

First of all, now that you're becoming a more joyful person and spreading that joy around your workplace, you're already off to a great start to make your customers truly happy. According to a May 2017 article on Forbes.com, happy employees make happy customers.[35] What happens on the inside of an organization is often felt on the outside by its customers. So, yay, you!

Second, Murray Goldstein of Cox Business wrote in ForbesVoice in October of 2015 that without satisfied customers, you're simply out of business.[36] Happy customers are loyal customers. He wrote that if you go above and beyond for them, you'll see real results with increased revenue. Retaining current customers is efficient and more profitable than seeking new ones. Loyal customers are also easier to sell to.

Goldstein continues by saying happy customers are more likely to recommend your company or product to others. With the Internet and social media driving so much business these days, this is crucial. Most business owners will tell you that word-of-mouth is the absolute best form of advertising since it doesn't require any time, effort, or money.

Finally, Goldstein talks about how happy customers can give you valuable feedback about your product or services. They can also tell you what you're doing right for customers and how you can do even better.

Entreprenuer.com sums up in March of 2013 why it's so important to bring joy to your customers in one sentence: Customer loyalty is hard to win and easy to lose.[37] That statement says so much I practically want to plaster it to my forehead.

Think about your own experiences as a customer. What restaurants, grocery stores, and drugstores do you frequent? Who is your doctor, dentist, optometrist, and mechanic? Their prices and products probably have something to do with why you go there so often - of course, what insurance you have comes into play with the medical professionals. But how do they treat you as a customer? Chances are, you're loyal to all of those places because they take those little extra steps to treat you well.

What about the places you'll never go to again? You probably have had the opposite experience there. We've all had those horror stories. One always rises to the top for me and my family.

Up until 2011, my husband and I took our vehicles to a small mom-and-pop auto repair shop in Central Indiana. The owner – we'll call him Sam – was quiet and nice enough, and his prices and service were good. In 2011 we noticed that our van was making a strange ticking sound. We took it to Sam's place a couple of times, but were reassured that our engine was fine and nothing was wrong. In fact, before taking a five hour drive (one way) to visit family over Labor Day weekend, we had Sam check it out one last time to make certain we would be safe on our trip.

When we were 90 minutes away from home as we returned to Indiana that Sunday night, the van's ticking noise turned into a terrible rumbling. John could barely pull over and get off onto an exit ramp, as we were on a busy highway heading east back to Indiana. Once we stopped, we couldn't get the van to start.

The only thing we could think to do was have a tow truck come to get us and the van back home. It took forever to find one willing to drive 90 minutes to Indiana and 90 minutes back. Finally, for $350, one company came and got us. John and I squeezed into the tow truck along with our two young sons and we finally got home at 1:30 in the morning.

Needless to say, we were extremely upset with Sam and his shop. The tow truck driver dropped off the van at Sam's shop, and I spoke with him on the phone the following Tuesday morning. My jaw dropped when he told me we needed a brand new engine.

After hearing our story, Sam feebly apologized to John and me. We were hoping to have at least free labor for the installation of the new engine or something substantial to make up for all we had been through, especially since we had been reassured over and over again that our van was fine for traveling. Sam did call around to get a refurbished engine for us, but that was the extent of things. After we got the new engine, we never returned to his shop again.

Despite our awful experience on the road, if Sam had sincerely apologized and gone above and beyond to make up for his shop's mistake, we actually might have stayed. Free oil changes for a year, a card with a hand written apology, a gift certificate to a nice restaurant, or just him taking the time to sit down with us to express how awful he felt would've made a tremendous difference. And I'm not even saying Sam is a bad guy. I just don't think he was ever taught how to do those little things to make his customers extremely happy.

Now I'll do a 180. When I worked for the Town of Field's Corner, we had a small medical clinic for employees and their families, which is common for many big companies and municipalities these days. My family liked the doctors and nurses there, but we absolutely adored one person in particular - Dr. Lily Kelly.

Dr. Kelly is one busy lady. Not only is she a doctor, which requires a ton of hard work and dedication, but when I was with the town she had three small children as well. When any of us would see her for a particular issue, we felt like we were talking to an old friend. Dr. Kelly asked many in-depth questions about our health and we never felt rushed. She remembered things about our lives, including our families and what we did in our jobs.

Whenever we saw Dr. Kelly and had to stay home from work, she would call us the evening after our appointments and ask how we were doing. Sometimes if the illness were really bad she would call again a couple days later to make certain we were improving! I swear, Dr. Kelly was the best part of being sick. We almost started to make up illnesses just to see her.

Seriously, though, when I left the town, what upset John and me the most was not being able to have Dr. Kelly as our physician any longer. We had planned to switch to her private practice even though she was 45 minutes away, but she had discontinued it and was only practicing in the city's clinic.

We liked Dr. Kelly so much that we sent her a card and flowers on my last day. Dr. Kelly was so touched. Here we are a few years later, and neither John nor I have found another family practitioner quite like her.

Folks, to be competitive, keep improving, and well, make more money (which is usually our goal!), we absolutely cannot ignore bringing joy to our customers. We can't just deliver what they expect, but must surprise them with the unexpected – in good ways! If we consistently make our customers happy, we'll feel the rewards for years to come. And just like what we talked about with spreading joy to your coworkers, most methods for bringing this joy are not difficult. In fact, they can often be fun for all parties! Let's dive in to the simple things we can do starting tomorrow to make our customers joyful.

Amy Thornton

"Listening is being able to be changed by the other person."
Alan Alda

Chapter Twelve

A Simple Way to Make Our Customers Smile

By now some of you may be thinking, "Wait a minute, I haven't read any tips lately for us introverts, or for those times I just don't really feel like doing much talking." Hallelujah, friends, this chapter is perfect for you!

One of the myths in our society is that to be a brilliant conversationalist, you have to be current on a variety of topics and ready to talk about anything. But really, the opposite is true. You don't have to know diddly-squat about current events to converse with customers and have them like you. And instead of being ready to talk about anything, be ready instead to *ask them questions* about anything.

One of my friends from the Central Indiana Dale Carnegie world always said, "God gave us two ears vs. one mouth for a reason." We can make connections with people and help them like us – and our companies or organizations - by listening to them. I mean HONESTLY listening to them, *with sincerity.*

To illustrate this point, let me take you to May of 2017. I had just quit my part-time job working for the soil and water conservation district to devote all of my time exclusively to the Link Observatory Space Science Institute. Right when I started this new adventure, some NASA representatives made plans to visit the observatory while they were in Indianapolis for a conference. Yes, you read that right, NASA, the National Aeronautics and Space Administration, a/k/a The Big Kahuna of All Things Space. Our director and deputy director invited me down to the observatory so I could be a part of the meeting to take place on a Monday evening. I jumped at the opportunity and even left my poor husband alone to plead our case for building the new garage to our local Board of Zoning appeals that night (he knocked it out of the park and they approved it, thankfully).

Right after I said "Oh yes, I'll definitely be there," I was struck with some big-time nerves. After all, I had only been a part-time contractor for the observatory up until that time. I didn't even have real business cards or a title yet! But I was determined to put my best foot forward. This meeting was an important step in the growth of our partnership with NASA and I wanted to do all I could to make it successful.

Of course I dressed my best, made certain to remove every bit of cat hair from my good coat – yes, it was May in Indiana but still chilly – and drove the full hour down while listening to motivational music. I was gonna be joyful and wow these people – screw my nerves!

Carol and Darren of NASA fame arrived at the observatory not long after I did. We gave them a brief tour before hopping into our cars and driving to Grey Brothers Cafeteria for dinner. Grey Brothers is *a legend* in Central Indiana. With delicious pieces of pie as big as your head and down-home cooking that tastes like what your grandma makes, it's no wonder.

While waiting in line to get our food, I asked Carol questions about where she grew up and how long she had been with NASA. I was surprised to hear that she was from the nearby town of Martinsville. As we sat down to eat, I asked her more questions and soon we all heard about her two pre-teen kiddos and her husband. Carol proudly showed us a locket with pictures of her son and daughter. She even took a few minutes away from dinner to call and tell them goodnight.

I inquired about how she became employed with NASA and learned that it all started with her role as a science teacher! Her path was fascinating and unbelievable.

Soon my attention was turned to Darren, who in addition to being a brilliant part of NASA's Digital Learning Network had a "side career" as a musician and DJ. He beamed while he produced pictures of his beautiful fiancé in South America and we all were intrigued with his story as well. Throughout dinner, we let both Carol and Darren tell us more about their lives and we had a delightful time.

We returned to the observatory and our directors presented our history, current activities, and goals. Carol and Darren were "wowed" by what they saw, as was I, despite having seen it all before. They left feeling excited to share what we had been doing with their co-workers and supervisors.

After they were on the road, I shook the director's hand and said that I thought the evening had gone well. He surprised me by saying, "Amy, whenever we're around you, we always learn how to interact better with others." I blushed, thanked him, and then climbed into my Mini Cooper, feeling somewhat stunned. That was one of the best compliments I had ever received. But it took me a little while to figure out how I had earned it.

I realized on my drive home that I had led almost the entire conversation before and during our dinner *simply by asking questions!* I'm a firm believer that everyone has a fascinating story to share with the world, and I like to hear as many of these as possible. By just being genuinely curious, asking Carol and Darren questions, and truly listening to them, they felt relaxed, comfortable, and as if they were with friends. We could tell that they enjoyed their evening immensely. This was confirmed when we received this enthusiastic email message from Carol the next morning:

It was such a pleasure to spend time with the four of you last night at the Link Observatory. I was overwhelmed with the history and the magnitude of the facility let alone your vision and goal for your program. It really is a stunning organization that you have and I am so excited that we are working towards an agreement to work in a more concerted effort to benefit us both.

Like many NASA employees, Carol is a busy person. I was amazed that she took the time to send us this thank you. This is just one example of what can happen when we ask questions and genuinely listen to our customers.

I see another example of people bringing joy to customers every time I visit my neighborhood bank. What's amazing is that this is a branch that wasn't welcome in our area in the beginning. They had to tear down a historic home in order to build it, which initially ruffled some feathers, including my own. But the bank's owner and founder sat down and met with neighbors like myself to get their thoughts and share the bank's plans. I was impressed from the start, and this branch soon became a positive addition to our neighborhood.

But the story doesn't end there. It continues to be a positive addition thanks to its two main tellers – Katie and Madison. I used to see them every day when I made deposits for the soil and water conservation district. They're so good with customers that I'm sad now that I don't see them as often.

Why? Because they ask questions and are sincerely interested in their customers. I not only witness this through my own interactions, but with those who are in line before me. I've gotten to know Katie so well that we've had lunch on occasion!

Katie and Madison often ask me about my sons, my husband, my house, my dogs, my work, my mom, and so many other topics. I think they know me better than some of my friends! It's no wonder that our family has opened multiple accounts there.

I want to challenge you to think of customers you'd like to bring joy to or customers you want to have an even better relationship with. If you often encounter new customers, you might be in a perfect place to ask just a couple of questions to bring them joy. Some that could work in either situation include:

"Have you lived in this area long?" if not, you can follow up with, "Where are you from? What was that city/town/area like?"

"Where do you work? What's it like?"

"So what brings you here today?" Many times people will tell you a story that can naturally lead to some questions.

A unique question I've heard recently and love is, "What types of things do you like to do?" It's not the same old "What do you do?" scenario that inevitably gets people just talking about their jobs. It opens up the possibility for someone to share some fascinating passions and hobbies with you. Most folks are eager to show the world what they're interested in.

PLEASE NOTE – this exercise is not meant to be an interrogation. Remember to breathe, pause, and see where the conversation goes naturally. Just a couple of questions are often all that are needed. Steer away from personal questions about family unless you know your customer well. Some people are shy and may not be comfortable talking with you more than necessary. It's important to watch your customer's body language to make certain they're relaxed and happy to be a part of the growing conversation. We'll cover more about body language in the next chapter.

Chances are, by showing interest in your customers and truly listening to what they're saying, you'll make their day as well as your own - and potentially increase your business!

"The most fundamental psychological need is to be appreciated."
William James, the father of psychology

Chapter Thirteen

Knock Their Socks off "Thank You's"

Do you feel appreciated as much as you should be in life? Chances are the answer is no. A lot of times we think this happens because our current world is so crazy and hectic. But I believe this has been going on since the dawn of time. Have you ever heard the story about Jesus healing the 10 lepers? In summary, Jesus told them all to show themselves to the priests after they had asked him to cure them. On their way to see the priests, all 10 were healed. Only one returned to Jesus to tell him thank you. Jesus asked, "Where are the other nine?" upon seeing him.

Appreciation is so powerful, and doing it well at work will help you retain customers and attract more in the future. Essentially, we want to knock their socks off! Let's delve into some simple, yet memorable, ways to accomplish this goal.

A Hand Written Note or Card

Like a real birthday card given to a coworker, a hand written thank you note or card stands out to a customer. It's so rare, but still costs little in terms of time and effort. If you own a company or have money in your department budget, invest in some simple thank you cards with your logo. If you are typically short on time, have them pre-printed with a short message such as "We appreciate your business and hope to see you again soon!" Make certain to always have at least one person sign it by hand.

If you can find that extra minute or two, write a personal message on a blank card. Some examples are:

"We know you have dozens of other options for your auto repair needs. We appreciate you trusting us and look forward to your next visit."

"Thank you so much for coming to see us today. Customers like you make us happy to do what we do."

"We appreciate your donation during this busy time of year! Thank you for making a difference."

"Thanks for stopping by!"

You can either give it to the customer in person once their visit is complete or mail it afterwards. In this world of email and online social media, getting a thank you note in the mail is so special. My jaw dropped the other day when I received a handwritten, mailed thank you note from Reggie's, our auto repair shop. The note was only two sentences and a signature, but I was still in disbelief that they took the time to write and send it.

I've always made certain to send a handwritten thank you card whenever the non-profit organization I work for receives a large donation or grant. I either write a message and sign the card or buy a thank you card with a message already in it and have the executive director and/or program staff members sign it. I'll never forget seeing one of my cards on a donor's desk months after we received their gift! Obviously it meant a lot to them that we took the time to send that hand written note.

Your thank you note can also do triple duty. It can not only show appreciation, but it can serve as a receipt AND an invitation for your customer to return soon.

Even a scribbled note of appreciation on a receipt can be special. I love when a waiter or waitress writes a simple "Thank you! It was a pleasure to serve you. We hope to see you again soon," on my receipt. Talk about a short and sweet example of a thank you note doing triple duty! It adds that human touch and reminds me that the evening wasn't just about food, but connecting with people. It also guarantees a bigger tip from me to that server!

Speaking of receipts, conversio.com, formally Receiptful, can help you create amazing, personalized receipts that make customers say, "wow!" They focus more on receipts for computers, phones, and other devices, but can still give you brilliant ideas for hand written messages. And on that topic, let's talk about online notes.

Creative Typed and Online Thank You Notes and Receipts

Your company might be so huge or time crunched that anything hand written just won't work. You can still get ahead of the competition by being original with your typed and online thank you notes and/or receipts.

When my friend Jennifer died five years ago after battling breast cancer, one of her final wishes was for people to send donations to the Dallas Zoo in her honor. You can imagine how big this organization is. I did some research and found out it's been around since 1888, is 106 acres, and is managed by the non-profit Dallas Zoological Society. Unfortunately, my family and I couldn't send a large donation at the time, but we wanted to do what we could to honor Jennifer. I sent them a $50 check and didn't give the zoo much thought after that.

Amy Thornton

Imagine my surprise a week later when I received one of the most creative, outstanding thank you notes/receipts ever in the mail. Here is an excerpt:

Please accept a huge gorilla-size thank you and gratitude for your contribution of $50 received on February 6, 2013. We're all going ape over your generosity.

Your gift will help our friends at the Dallas Zoological Society meet all the needs of our growing animal family.

Contented purrs from the cheetahs, toothy smiles from Nile crocodiles, and two-wing salutes from the Rock at Travis and Zach's Bird Landing are just a few of the ways you may see a show of appreciation for those who help our herds. That's just our nature.

On behalf of all the animals in our Dallas Zoo kingdom, we thank you for playing an important role in the success of your zoo.

Many bananas to you,

Patrick Gorilla, President, Board of Animals (And then signed with a gorilla hand print of course.)

At the bottom of the letter was a small box that served as my tax receipt. The box ended by saying "If you have any suggestions or want to talk to a human, please call me at the following number." It was signed by the development director.

I love this note so much that I use it as an example when I give my "Knock Their Socks off Thank You's" presentation at professional grant professional conferences. I plan to visit the zoo the next time I'm in the Dallas area!

The note beautifully illustrates why we need to focus on the customer in what we write – we need to talk about the WHO vs. the what. It's also an example of how a thank you note should make the funder feel good and give details, painting a picture if possible. The note should sound like you're speaking to the customer and should be as heartfelt as possible. You can add a contact name and phone number/email as well as a "P.S." telling the customer what's coming ahead in the future, such as a special sale or discount.

Make your thank you letter readable using short paragraphs, an easy to read font, and a ragged right margin. Studies show that a ragged right margin versus a right justified one is easier on the eyes.

If you need help in the creativity arena, several online sites in addition to conversio.com can help you with different phrases for your typed thank you notes. These include Shutterfly, Hallmark, and Pinterest. If possible, make the language fit your line of business like the Dallas Zoo does so well.

This extra effort will keep those customers coming back and they'll probably spread the word about your "genius" thank you notes!

Send or Share a Photo

This thank you method is probably the simplest of all, but it is my favorite way to show appreciation to customers - or really, anyone! Whenever my kids have a birthday party with friends, I always take their picture as they open each gift. We print out the photos and my boys write their thank you notes on the back of them. Sharing the happy smiles on Jonathon or Jacob's face with the gift giver's family is always appreciated!

When I worked for the Town of Field's Corner, I ordered a large "thank you" sign from our local sign and banner establishment. At the time it cost $30. Whenever we received a grant for a piece of equipment, project, or program, I would gather the appropriate staff members to have them hold that sign and take their picture. This was especially helpful for those types of projects that weren't "sexy," like the funding we received for a methane-powered boiler for our wastewater department. I then emailed the picture to the donor along with a brief, "Thanks to you, we did ABC," type of message.

In the boiler example, I wrote "Thanks to you, our waste water department is reducing its energy consumption by 10 to 20% each year." That may not sound impressive, but to the Indiana Office of Energy Development, it was exciting! We also posted the photo to the city's various social media outlets.

In 2017, the Link Institute received a $10,000 grant from the SIA Foundation to purchase two solar telescopes. These telescopes enable students and the general public to do something their mamas always told them not to do - stare at the sun (safely!). Having these telescopes enabled us to expand the number of people who could experience Heliophysics, which is the study of the sun. Since the total solar eclipse across America was about to occur that summer in August, all Institute staff members were quite busy using this equipment at various schools and events. I took photos of people enjoying the solar telescopes and emailed them regularly to my contact at the foundation. She was thrilled to see how much people were using and enjoying them.

With most of us having cell phones and connectivity to email or social media these days, we can use the power of pictures to show appreciation to customers and make them feel good about working with us!

Show Versus Tell

The Link Institute director and deputy director took our appreciation of the SIA Foundation to a whole other level. This foundation likes to host a breakfast twice a year for its grant recipients so they can share the difference they're making in their communities with each other. Our directors not only attended this breakfast and shared our stories on behalf of the Institute, but they brought the solar telescopes for attendees to enjoy after the event's conclusion. This was so brilliant, and I didn't even tell them to do it!

The weather happened to cooperate and provide some sunshine that morning, so SIA Foundation staff, board members, and event attendees all got to peek through the telescopes and safely view the sun. They were able to see sunspots, solar flares, and prominences, something most people never get to view with the naked eye. Not surprisingly, visits to the observatory increased a bit after this breakfast!

If there's any way to *show* a customer how much of an impact they're making versus just telling them, take advantage of it. Here are some ideas:

1. If you're a nonprofit, host an open house one day where your donors can see programs they helped fund in action. Serve a couple of light, easy refreshments. At Agapé Therapeutic Riding Resources just northeast of Indianapolis, donors and visitors can stop by anytime and look through a large window to see a therapeutic horseback riding session. They can't help but see the smiles, improved

muscular coordination, and progress of the riders - young, old, and in between.
2. Perhaps your business has experienced tremendous growth. Give your existing customers the chance to have a "sneak preview" one evening of, for example, the new physical therapy wing in your building. Customers can see where they and others will receive more advanced care than ever before.
3. Customer site visits for a variety of places can be fun for everyone involved. If you manufacture a product, open your door once a month for some guided public tours. Not only can you thank the public for its support of your business, but you can give them some eye-opening education as well.

All of these "show vs. tell" activities can be fairly simple to coordinate. You're performing your daily or evening work anyway, so why not invite some visitors to see what you do a couple of times a year?

News Releases/Social Media

This thank you method might be appropriate for only specific types of industries or organizations, but it's a simple one if you have a public relations person or department. If you're a nonprofit organization and a donor is giving you a significant amount of money, you can take a photo of them handing a check to your staff or board and send it out to the local media along with a brief news article. You can also post the picture to social media. This method does double duty, as it is another way to thank someone, but it also exposes what is great about your organization and what you do specifically for the community.

Mention Customers in an Annual Report or Newsletter

Some of us older folks might remember the excitement of seeing our photo and an article about us in the local paper growing up. It was always a thrill to open up the newspaper and see myself on stage in my high school play, on the tennis court during an intense match, or leading a fundraiser in college.

Why not feature customers in your annual report or newsletter? If you have way too many customers to mention them all, you can do a "customer of the year" or "customer of the month" corner with a photo and brief paragraph. You can do a 5 to 10 minute interview of the person to help you write their story, then share why they were selected for this honor within your company. Most people will love the attention and it's a fun way to tell the whole world how much you appreciate them.

Artwork/Thank You from Children or Clients Served

Once again, this might only work for certain workplaces, but sharing artwork or thank you notes from children or clients served all because of your customers is one of the most memorable ways to show appreciation. The therapeutic horseback riding center I mentioned previously had a lot of fun working with their young riders to create drawings to share with donors. It only took 10 minutes during their classroom sessions to draw these pictures with crayons and markers, but their effect on donors lasted much longer.

Children aren't the only ones that can have fun with this. Maybe you work for a business or organization that serves a variety of ages such as a hospital or a rehabilitation facility. You can have patients and clients draw "before" and "after" pictures illustrating how they felt before their treatment/therapy and after. Stress to them that they don't have to be Picassos for this project. Even simple stick figures get the point across (if you've ever played Pictionary you know what I mean).

If markers and crayons won't do the trick, how about letting children or others who have benefited from a donor or customer write a thank you note? It could start out by saying "Thanks to you, I..." with the client listing the ways he or she has improved. Some examples could include:

"Thanks to you, I am finally regaining my speech. I was able to tell my son hello yesterday for the first time in months."

"Thanks to you, the hospital's new CAT scan machine detected my cancer early and I was able to beat it."

"Thanks to you, I can walk again and play with my big sister."

This also takes just minutes, but it really hits home with donors and customers and reminds them why they chose to help your business or organization.

Tree or Shrub Planting with Small Recognition Sign

If you do any sort of yearly improvements for your landscaping, this is almost a no-brainer. When you plant that new tree or shrub, why not order a durable outdoor plaque recognizing an outstanding customer to be placed in front of it? You can make this a big deal and mention it in a news release, report, social media, or newsletter; or you can wait and surprise that special customer the next time they visit. This type of recognition certainly would appeal to anyone with a green thumb!

Now that I've shared easy ways to show appreciation to customers, it's time to delve into some efforts that require a little more time and money to reap even greater rewards. (Psst - they're also a blast!)

Thank-a-Thons

Remember a good old-fashioned phone call from a real human being? This concept is starting to disappear in our society. With more texting, emails, and the occasional "robo/telemarketing/scam" call, sadly, talking to someone on the phone is not as great as it used to be. Thank-a-thons can bring that positivity back!

A thank-a-thon involves a group of people such as staff or board members from an organization or business making phone calls of appreciation to customers. Everyone usually calls 5 to 10 customers with a short script that goes something like this:

"Hello, Mr./Mrs./Ms. Smith? This is Amy from ABC. We wanted to take a minute today to call and personally thank you for your recent donation/purchase/visit with us. It's already making such a difference and we appreciate you very much."

Then, they stop talking.

Chances are, your customer will be flabbergasted if you actually reach them versus their voicemail. This was the case with me recently when someone from Reggie's called just to thank me for my business after an oil change. A simple, inexpensive oil change!

"Uh... you're welcome," I replied in surprise.

"Is your Mini Cooper doing well after your visit with us?" For a moment I felt like this woman was talking about one of my children, she sounded so sincere.

"Yes, absolutely." I proceeded to thank her for the phone call and tell her how amazed I was to receive it. She said they were trying out personalized thank you calls. I told her the idea was brilliant.

Thank-a-thons can take place once a month with everyone in the same building or each person can take a day to make his or her calls. Or someone can make one phone call a day if time is short. They're such a simple way to spread joy to customers. And after the initial script, the caller can sit back and listen to the response. If you're the one making the call, you might hear something interesting to help improve your business or receive a testimonial that you can share on social media or elsewhere - with permission of course.

How about having a business owner, manager, director, or someone else in a high position call and thank a customer once in a while? Can you imagine how good that would make someone feel to have, for example, a founder of a company call and share his or her appreciation for a minute?

No matter who makes that call, even if it just goes to voicemail, know that it may be a welcome relief to hear and it might make someone's day. People won't easily forget your sincere phone call of appreciation!

Joy to You and Me (At Work!)

The Way to a Customer's Heart is Through His (or Her) Stomach

Another way to show appreciation to customers is through food. And what's better than breakfast – the most important meal of the day! Spread the word on social media, email, newsletters, or other avenues that you're hosting a free annual "grab and go" breakfast to thank your customers. Keep things simple by serving a variety of bagels, coffee, juice, tea, and fruit. Host it in an easy, accessible location where customers can park, stay and chat awhile if they like, or simply grab a bag and their favorite morning beverage and be on their way.

You may want to offer curbside pick-up so customers don't even have to leave their car. The point is to roll out the red carpet for your customers so they will want to attend. Just like most big events in life, you probably won't have more than a third to half of your regular customers attending due to their work or other commitments. But just knowing you're providing a special breakfast can show the world how you go above and beyond for your customers.

Once again, Reggie's has also conquered this area of appreciation. My jaw dropped when I picked up my car for the first time and they handed me two cookies from my favorite bakery in town. We're talking lemon bars - delightful, ooey-gooey squares of Heaven! My kids practically start drooling when they know my car has to go in for maintenance now.

What about those nice bank tellers who always have the suckers for kids - or kids at heart! And now they sometimes pass through dog biscuits in the drive-through tube when they see a customer's furry companion in the window! Happy kids AND dogs? That's just a win-win right there.

Wall or Plaque of Fame

If you frequently see your customers throughout the day, why not create a "Wall of Fame," showing off a customer of the month? You can select a customer of the month for numerous reasons:

1. Host a writing contest where you invite your customers to share why they love your products or services. This also gives you great testimonial material for your business!
2. If you have records of how long someone has been doing business with you, you can randomly select individuals who have been working with you for a certain number of months or years.
3. If you know your customers well, maybe you can highlight those individuals who are doing awesome volunteer work and making a difference for others.
4. Look up the previous month's receipts and select the individual who gave you the most revenue.

After you let your customer know he or she is this month's winner, simply take their photo (if they are OK with it of course), create a template you can use over and over again, place the picture in the middle, and hang it on your wall where lots of people will see it.

You can also buy a plaque each year with space for all 12 months and add a customer name each month using the same methods previously mentioned.

As we draw to a close in this section, just remember, like all of the steps discussed in this book, to take things one at a time when exploring new ways to show appreciation to customers. If you've never gone above and beyond to thank your customers, start slowly with one or two new methods. Divide and conquer as well, as many of these concepts can be implemented by several different employees. Some methods might appeal to one type of employee more than another.

Be prepared as you slowly build your arsenal of appreciation, however, to increase your business like nothing you've ever done before. You'll begin to feel incredibly warm and fuzzy., gain an unbelievable number of new customers, and leave a lasting impression upon your existing customers that will have them talking about you fondly for years to come!

Amy Thornton

"There is no such thing as a pure extrovert or pure introvert. Such a man (woman) would be in a lunatic asylum." Jung, founder of analytical psychology in the development of extroversion – introversion theory.

Chapter Fourteen

Just Keep Smilin' and Trust Your Gut

Do you remember certain employees we discussed who just won't appreciate or even want your efforts to bring them joy at work? You'll run into the same situation with customers. Sometimes customers just want to get in, make a purchase, and get out. They may be introverted and simply don't care for attention, or they just may be busy and don't have time for you to show them that special appreciation or care. Or maybe they're passing through town and will never see you again.

Some may be uncomfortable with questions or long periods of eye contact. The key here is to watch your customer's body language or simply ask them if they need anything. If they say they're fine, then move on and continue with your other duties.

I'll never forget the time my husband, our sons, and I sat down to dinner at Disney World's Animal Kingdom during parade time. We had experienced a wonderful, exciting day and were looking forward to relaxing and finally getting something to eat. All four of us were also tired, thus the main reason we were missing the parade. We just wanted to spend some quiet time together with a meal.

Our waiter was tall, young, blond, and handsome. And talkative. We had the restaurant to ourselves, which we figured meant we'd have quick service. We didn't think we would have babbly service.

Don't get me wrong - my husband and I love to talk to people when we go out to eat. We usually learn our server's name and a little bit about them. Of course we're always polite and friendly. But our server typically leaves the table after taking our orders and after delivering the beverages and food. He or she will check to see how things are later and then go on to other tables. The server doesn't linger at the table and chatter. Constantly.

But this guy would not leave us alone. He talked to us about where we were from, the weather, Animal Kingdom, what was happening at Animal Kingdom, the restaurant itself, what he had been up to that day... it went on and on. Jonathon and Jacob, who were six and seven at the time, kept squirming in their seats. John and I fidgeted and tried to turn our attention to the menus, the restaurant itself, *anything* but this waiter.

"Hmmm, we'd better let you get back to your work," I finally said in desperation, my eyes darting to the kitchen, "I'm sure you'll be hopping once this parade is over."

The waiter finally left when it was time to get our food. All four of us just stared at each other, contemplating whether we should make a run for it. Needless to say, after we were finished with dinner we got the heck out of there before Mr. Chatty could bother us some more.

There's a big difference between spreading joy to a customer and smothering them. Start out with a smile and a little effort such as saying, "Good Morning!" Then follow up by asking if they need any help or if they found what they were looking for. If you get a smile and a warm greeting in return, awesome. If you get good eye contact from the customer, that's a great signal for more engagement.

If your customer is looking at their phone more than you, crossing their arms, fidgeting, darting their eyes away from you constantly, or just plain scowling, that's your message saying it's time to back off! And if they do make a purchase from you, give them a polite thank you and let them be on their way.

If you run into this type of customer, don't take it personally. Smile, trust your gut, give the customer what they need, and move on. Chances are the next person will love the joy you shower upon them.

Amy Thornton

"Networking is marketing. Marketing yourself, marketing your uniqueness, marketing what you stand for."
Christine Comaford-Lynch

Part Four

Bringing Joy in Our Networking

Chapter Fifteen

Why We Should Bring Joy to Networking

Networking. Love it or hate it, it's something we do all the time without even realizing it and often without being in a formal event. Networking is critical not only when we are job hunting, but in every step of your career. Career Addict had a great article in May 2017 written by Mariliza Karrera that lists 10 important benefits of networking.[38] They are:

1. Networking allows you to help others.
2. It's a great way to exchange fresh ideas.
3. Networking makes you more visible.
4. It opens doors to new opportunities.
5. Networking allows you to express opinions.
6. It expands your support network.
7. Networking can help get you promoted.
8. It boosts your self-esteem.
9. Networking becomes your resource.
10. You can positively influence things.

Despite all of these great benefits, I know networking is still a challenge for many of us, especially if you are going to an event and you don't know a soul. Before we talk about how to bring joy to the experience, let's discuss how to calm our nerves before, during, and after a networking situation in order to do well.

In a May 2015 article from the Connecting Experts, author Penny Brenden, "The Networking Queen" shares these terrific tips. [39]

Before the Event

Pre-network to make early contacts. If you can find the event on social media or if there's a way to locate the attendee list online, reach out to a couple of people ahead of time. Penny says one of the most obvious people to contact is the host. You can let him or her know that you haven't met anyone at this event before. The host will probably be glad to introduce you to people once you arrive.

This is exactly what happened to me when I attended an Institute for Exceptional Education (IEE) networking event in December 2017. I had met the host, Mario, in September of that year when I showed him the Link Institute's educational products. Just minutes after arriving at the brewery where the event was to take place, Mario introduced me to three people and told them a bit about what the Institute did for schools. I was off and running. The two hours flew by as I talked to dozens of people and thoroughly enjoyed myself.

Practice your elevator speech. If you're not familiar with what an elevator speech is, it's a 30 second summary of your business or organization that will compel the listener to want to learn more. Once you have this summary, practice it out loud. Reading something in your head sounds quite different from hearing it spoken. If you practice your elevator speech over and over, it will be on the tip of your tongue and you'll be ready when someone approaches you.

<u>Set attainable goals.</u> Sure, you need to get out of your comfort zone at least a little, but you don't want to set the bar too high. You also need to give yourself an exit time. At the IEE event, I gave myself two hours to accomplish my goals of making four or five quality contacts. I'm happy to report I did just that in my timeframe.

During the Event

<u>Try to get your mind off yourself and focus on others instead.</u> I'll elaborate on this more later, but thinking about other people instead of yourself will almost guarantee you success. Once you've gotten to know someone, introduce them to a new person.

<u>Be yourself.</u> I already know that you're an awesome person. How am I so sure of this? You selected this book and have read it up to this point. If you didn't give a hoot about helping others, this book would not have appealed to you. You are reading it to not only bring positivity to yourself, but to those you work with. Heck, now I really want to meet you! So I know others will as well. And don't put yourself down. A little self-deprecating humor is fine, but people need to see the true you when networking.

<u>Be confident inside and out.</u> Penny brings up the age-old saying "Fake it 'til you make it," and in this situation it works. If you stand tall, smile, and give firm handshakes, you're already on the road to looking and being confident. And please give yourself a good pep talk. Don't talk down to yourself in this or any other situation.

After the Event

<u>Prioritize your follow up plan.</u> I always allow at least an hour the next day for follow up time after the event. That way, the people I met are fresh in my mind and I can select the top ones that I can help or who can help me. Sometimes I'll follow up via email, at other times I'll use social media, or I'll reach out via text. It all depends on the age and technology level of the individual I met. Remember, you want to build a positive, mutually beneficial relationship.

<u>Keep going to networking events!</u> You'll never get better at these things unless you go to them often. I try to attend a networking event at least once a month. Nowadays, I consider them to be a lot of fun and well worth my time. That wasn't always the case for me.

Networking Without Events

As I mentioned earlier, networking doesn't always involve going to a formal event. I never thought about this until I became a Dale Carnegie instructor. We were told right away in our training that we weren't just instructors when we were in the classroom. We had to practice what we preached at all times, which were good people skills. Once I thought about it this made perfect sense. The more we taught the course, the higher the chances we would run into current or former class members in the community. We had to be the face of Dale Carnegie wherever we went.

So many of us wear uniforms, lanyards, and name tags for work. We often go out to lunch or run errands before or after work. We are still the faces of our companies during this time. Sometimes we may not want to be, but that's the reality. These are great opportunities to network with others. People notice logos and company names and may ask you about your workplace and what you do. This is a great opportunity for your elevator speech.

When I first became a grant consultant and had my own business, I carried my business cards everywhere. Most of the time, it paid off, especially when I was volunteering at community events. It's natural for people to ask what you do when you first meet them. Having my card helped me easily spread the word and grow my business.

With the rise of social media, you don't even have to network face-to-face anymore, although I hope we never lose those opportunities in the future. In fact, social media helped me get to where I am today. When I went out completely on my own to do grant consulting, I posted that I was looking for clients on Facebook. One of my friends from college, Micah, messaged me the next day and told me that the Link Institute was looking for help with grant proposals. The rest is history!

Now we know why networking is so important and how to do it well. Let's move on to talk about ways to make it joyful for us and for those we meet.

First, make your appearance match the occasion. I say, go all out for it. You may be tired, especially if it's an evening event after a long day at work, but taking 10 minutes to put on some different clothes, brush your hair, and/or freshen up your make up if you're a woman can instantly perk you up. It's been said before, if you look good, you'll feel good.

Find some great music to enjoy on the drive to the event to get you in a positive mood or play it in your hotel room if you're away from home. Imagine that you're already at the event. Picture yourself smiling, laughing, and relaxed. What you "see" will be!

Sometimes when I dread a networking event - and yes, this still happens on occasion - I remind myself that almost every time I go to one of them, something unexpectedly wonderful happens. Open yourself up to what the universe is going to provide in the next few hours. You might meet someone who needs exactly what you or your company has to offer. Remind yourself of past success in networking. Rejoice in that moment.

Will there be food or drinks at the meeting place? Woo hoo! This is always extra cause for celebration, especially in my case. I may not drink alcohol, but I've always loved food. At different networking sessions at my last National Grant Professional Association conference in San Diego, I not only enjoyed the company, but the California food was delectable and healthy. Another win-win! You may have the same experience at this next event.

Just remember that even though a lot of evening networking events are similar to parties, be careful how much alcohol you consume. Most of us get a little fuzzy-brained and we don't say the most intelligent things when we've indulged too much. Know your limit and stick to it!

Once the event is over and you're back at work, at home, or in your hotel room, congratulate yourself on a successful evening. Did you make at least one great contact or help another person in some way? That's a success that you should feel good about.

Joy to You and Me (At Work!)

Since you've adjusted your mindset and you're ready to have the most joyful experience in networking, now it's time to bring joy to others at these events. My number one piece of advice is what I alluded to earlier - focus on other people throughout most of the event. Don't worry that you won't promote your company or yourself with this mindset. People will naturally ask you questions as the event continues.

By now you've noticed a pattern throughout this book and it also extends to networking. It bears repeating - one of the best ways to bring joy to others is to listen to them. Don't think about what you'll say next. Instead, truly *hear* what others are telling you. Lean in to hear them better if you have to or move to a quieter spot, maintain eye contact, and open up your mind to what you can learn from that other person. It might not relate in any way, shape, or form to what you do. But you may be able to connect that person to someone you know or to another company that can help them.

Once again, ask questions. Forbes has a great article from May 2016 listing 10 awesome questions to ask at a networking event.[40] They are:

1. Where do you recommend I go while I'm here? This one is perfect for when you have traveled out of town for an event. The locals will enjoy telling you about some great spots that are off the beaten path. This is how I found the best Mexican restaurant I've ever been to when I was in San Diego.
2. How did you hear about this event?
3. What is on your reading list? The answer to this question alone could get me talking for hours!

4. What is your favorite thing to do? This is similar to what I mentioned in the section about asking questions to customers. People love to talk about their hobbies!
5. Where are you from? This could lead to other questions such as where did you go to college, trade school, or other training?
6. What did you think about the event? Obviously this one is good towards the end of or after the session.
7. What is your story? I can't tell you how much I love this one. I've shared with you that thanks to instructing the Dale Carnegie Course, I discovered that everyone has a story. Most of the time it's fascinating and I love learning about other people's lives. I think you will, too.
8. How did you decide to do what you do? This usually leads to a story about a pivotal life experience.
9. What are some of your "go to" resources for getting guidance about your field of work? This is an obvious way for you to gain some great ideas for your own career.
10. How can I be helpful to you right now? Wow. Talk about a question that shows how much you want to help others! People will be pleasantly surprised by this one.

By asking good questions and sincerely listening to people throughout the event you will literally draw people to you. They will enjoy meeting and speaking with you. And you'll discover the more you bring joy to others in networking, the more fun you'll have. You may make some great new friends, as I have through my Grant Professionals Association.

Speaking of - let me share a story with you. In the summer of 2015, a woman by the name of Anna Duncan contacted me out of the blue to see if I wanted to meet her for lunch. She and I had talked briefly at grant professional meetings, but had never really gotten to know one another.

At first I hesitated. Like so many people these days, I was busy that summer not only professionally, but personally. I wondered why on earth I should take a couple hours out of my day to go meet her for lunch when we barely knew each other. But my gut said to give it a whirl.

I met Anna at a pizza place and we practically had the restaurant to ourselves. Within five minutes, I realized what an absolute delight she was. We made plans to attend the regional grant professional conference that fall in Ohio, which was just 2-1/2 hours away. Due to a recent foot surgery that Anna had, I drove to and from the conference that September.

I don't think a road trip has ever gone faster for me. Anna and I discovered several important things that we both had in common. I loved hearing all about her family, friends, experiences growing up, and career. We exchanged lots of stories about our grant proposal ups and downs. And we enjoyed attending the conference together.

Today, Anna is one of my closest friends. I helped her get her current job. She helped me to become a hoop dance instructor in 2016, which had been a dream of mine for years. We check in on each other once in awhile via email and text. We meet almost every month for lunch and always give each other tremendous joy.

When I think back to what I would have missed out on if I had told her "no" back in the summer of 2015, I almost get teary-eyed.

You may never gain a close friend like I did through networking, but you might get your "circle" - people who understand about the ups and downs of your job better than anyone else. I always refer to my friends and colleagues at the Grant Professionals Association as "my peeps" and I'm glad to have them in my life.

So be open to whatever might come your way through networking. And if you have a good sense of humor, feel free to throw that into an event once in a while. When I attended the Uptown Group last summer, a network of people and businesses on the north side of Indianapolis, I didn't know a single soul. But I was determined to have fun on that beautiful, warm summer evening and was pleased to discover that the event was taking place outdoors on the patio of a quaint little winery.

The group was jovial and relaxed. At one point a gal by the name of Angie began to talk about her family. After sharing the recent antics of her many children, she ended by teasingly stating, "You know, smart people have four kids or more." To which I replied, "Well, I guess I'll stay dumb." I was pleased to get some good laughs out of that one.

By doing some prep work to psych yourself up for these events, listening and focusing on bringing joy to others while networking, and appreciating all the wonderful benefits these opportunities have to offer, you'll advance yourself and your company into some "out of this world" territory. I'm talking beyond *anything* you could ever have conceived.

And instead of dreading that next networking session, you'll be eager and ready to jump in to make it memorable for everyone you come in contact with!

Joy to You and Me (At Work!)

"I don't trust anyone who doesn't laugh." *Maya Angelou*

Chapter Sixteen

Don't Lose the Fun

Joyful workplaces perform better than others. They're more productive, less stressful, more energetic, and downright fun. They attract fresh talent. People who work in a positive company or organization look forward to their jobs and usually want to stick around. These companies stand out, grow, and often beat the competition. Joyful work places don't just keep the positivity on the inside – they spread it to their customers and to everyone they come in contact with.

After reading this book and learning from the research, stories, and examples of how to bring joy to the workplace, I must leave you with an important final point. Once you have that positivity at work, you and hopefully the others you've spread that joy to must make a commitment to ensure it continues and grows for years - no, hopefully decades - to come.

Don't put this book down along with your notes and forget everything. Start your plan tomorrow, even if it's just a small step, and don't let up. Mark your calendar to remind yourself to bring joy to your surroundings, to a coworker, to a customer, and/or to a networking event at least once week. Set up weekly, monthly, or yearly reminders until bringing joy becomes a habit.

To illustrate why this is so important, let me tell you about Organization A and Organization B. I'd love to give you real names, since these are true stories, but of course I must always protect the innocent! I worked for both organizations and did my best to bring joy to them. One other coworker at Organization A did the same thing.

Organization A had frequent potlucks either at breakfast or lunch to celebrate birthdays and holidays. My department would often post signs in the break room to honor certain milestones. We enjoyed birthday cakes, donuts, king cakes for Mardi Gras, angel food cake, homemade pies, and other sweets at least every other week. The occasional fun prank popped up to send us into gales of laughter. We made certain to pass around and sign a card whenever someone had a birthday or other special celebration.

And by now you know me and what I typically add to the mix. Our celebrations often included singing, goofy poems, "On the day you were born" readings, decorations galore, and numerous gag gifts.

I also remember two employees in particular having the most distinctive laughs throughout the day. I loved to hear them echo down the hallway.

I looked forward to going into Organization A every morning unless I was extremely tired or not feeling well. Everyone in our department did their best each day, but had a lot of fun, too.

As time went on, the other joyful coworker and I moved on to different organizations. But I still kept in touch with a couple of ladies from my department. I left them funny voicemails for their birthdays to keep up on tradition.

I went out to lunch with the two of them about a year after I had left. As we were diving into our chips and salsa and catching up, I asked if they were still continuing with the fun celebrations and pranks. Their faces fell.

"No, not really," one friend said. "I'm afraid we just go in, do our jobs, and go home. Every day." My heart sank upon hearing this.

"Wait, now come on," I replied, "You all aren't doing anything, not even a potluck on occasion?" Both of my friends shook their heads.

"Since the two of you left, things just aren't the same," my other friend said. "It's all work and no fun." I felt terribly sad to hear this news.

When I visited my old department afterwards, I could actually feel a difference. The suite was quiet, with no laughter to be heard. Everyone was certainly professional, but the light-hearted feeling had disappeared. There wasn't a flower, dessert, or colorful decoration to be found. This was such a stark contrast to me compared to how things had been, and I left feeling depressed for my former coworkers.

Organization B was also a joyful place, though much smaller in scale. While I was only there for about 15 months, I implemented my positive practices right from the start. We had a great time celebrating everything from Administrative Professionals Day, to Boss's Day, to Halloween and Christmas. I interacted with more customers face to face at this organization, and had a blast getting to know them all. I wrote about some of them in our newsletters and always listened to what they had to say with interest. We also offered coloring books for kids who came in with their parents.

This was my favorite place for funny emails. My coworkers quickly got into the spirit and were often more creative than me! Somehow a "carrot mascot" became a theme for weeks. And the pranks were some of the best I've ever been proud to be a part - or victim - of.

My joyful practices quickly rubbed off on everyone. One coworker printed off an awesome sign for me on my birthday. Then she had a good laugh when I was so incredibly busy that day I didn't even notice it until after lunch! I got a hilarious card later on with rather outrageous, creative signatures. And when we took a break for my birthday dessert, it was one of the most delicious treats I've ever had.

When I left this organization for a better opportunity, I enjoyed everyone so much I stayed in contact with all of them. I wondered if they would keep up the positive, wonderful traditions we had all started together.

Imagine my delight when I visited six weeks later for a breakfast celebration for one gal's birthday. A huge sign with everyone's signatures was posted on her office door. We enjoyed her favorite breakfast sweets and laughed when she opened up her card and gag gifts. I could tell when I left she was going to have an excellent day.

I continued to hear stories about the fun they kept on having and was even privy to a few uproarious emails. And imagine my surprise when I received a funny card in the mail from all of them three months later for my birthday. The signatures were the stuff of legends.

As I write this, I've made plans to go to Organization B's annual meeting in a couple of weeks even though it doesn't apply to my current work. Why? Because I am now their customer and their joy still spreads to me. I know their annual meeting will be both informative and positive and I can't wait to see everyone again!

Joy to You and Me (At Work!)

As we approach the end of this joyful journey, I want to stress to you that once you've brought joy to the workplace, you must never lose it. You have to do all you can to leave a legacy of positivity if you move on to a different position. I didn't encourage Organization A to keep doing positive things. It simply wasn't on my radar. But after seeing and hearing about the lack of joy there, I did ask (or beg!) Organization B to never lose the fun. The difference in both atmospheres after I left was astonishing.

As I said in the beginning, you don't have to do every single thing in this book in order to make a difference both in and outside of your workplace. Pick what's right for you and what's appropriate for where you work. But don't forget to sneak outside your comfort zone once in a while! That's how we all stretch and grow in life.

I firmly believe the more joy we can spread to our workplaces, the happier we'll all be. I wish you much joy and love on this journey of positivity and would also like to hear your stories. Let me know if you try something from this book and how things turn out! I thank you for reading it and making a commitment to spreading happiness while on the job.

Book Discussion Questions

1. How did you feel about networking before reading this book? Do you feel differently now? Why or why not?

2. Who are your customers? How do you thank them currently? Were you inspired after reading this book to try some new ways to show them appreciation? If so, what are the first things you'll do?

3. Do you work with someone like "The Wall?" Do you handle that person using one of the methods listed in the book or do you approach things differently? How have those methods worked or not worked for you?

4. What's the nicest thing anyone's ever done for you when you left a company? Or started with one? How did that action make you feel? Did it inspire you to do similar things for others? Why or why not?

5. What was your biggest "a-ha!" moment when reading about ways you can start to be more joyful at work (i.e., better voice mail greeting, improving your surroundings, etc.)? Did you discover some habits you can improve or implement that will start to help you right away? Why or why not?

6. Exercising, eating right, getting enough sleep, volunteering, and praying (or speaking to "the universe") are all ways to help us be our happiest, most joyful selves. Which one(s) do

you struggle with the most? How can you improve in those areas?

7. The author shares several ideas about how to celebrate different occasions in the workplace. What ones have you done or would like to do that are different from the book? For example, one reader shared that she'd love to host a breakfast for employees and their children. She thought a "Donuts with Dad" or "Donuts with Mom" Day would be fun and would give children a glimpse of what a "grown up" workday is like.

About the Author

Amy has been bringing joy to her workplaces for over 25 years thanks to her innate enthusiasm and extensive training on how to spread it to others for the improvement of all. Shankland was an instructor for the Dale Carnegie Human Relations Course for over a decade. She has won several awards for the enthusiasm she shares with both co-workers and customers.

Amy Thornton Shankland loves to write and is a former columnist for the Noblesville Daily Times, freelance writer for Indy's Child, and editor for her church's bulletin. She also created an "Enthusiastic Mama" blog that ran from 2015 -2016.

She self-published and promoted a novel called Hoop Mama in 2013 through Fast Pencil.

She has given local, regional, and national workshops on various writing topics thanks to her 15+ years as a grant professional.

Shankland lives near Indianapolis with her husband, two sons, two dogs, and two cats. She enjoys volunteering for various local organizations, hoop dancing, reading, and walking everywhere she possibly can.

Wanna Learn More?

I highly recommend the following publications and courses to help you continue to bring joy to the workplace. All of these have changed my life for the better and I believe they'll help you, too!

How to Win Friends and Influence People, Dale Carnegie (Carnegie, Dale. *How to Win Friends and Influence People.* New York, NY. Simon & Schuster. 1936.)

You've already heard me refer to this book and the course it generated. Mr. Carnegie wrote more books on topics such as how to conquer worry; public speaking; leadership; and many others to help people succeed both personally and professionally.

Dale Carnegie courses are offered in person and online throughout the United States and beyond as well. They include leadership development and personal, sales, and presentation effectiveness. To find what's available near you, go to

www.dalecarnegie.com

Do It Well, Make It Fun, Ron Culbertson (Culbertson, Ron. *Do It Well, Make It Fun.* Austin, TX. Greenleaf Book Group Press. 2012.)

This book helped me expand the joyful things I was already doing at work and to get even more creative. The author has a wonderful sense of humor and you'll enjoy his tips on how to have fun while being tremendously productive.

Quench Your Own Thirst, Jim Koch (Koch, Jim. *Quench Your Own Thirst.* New York, NY. Flatiron Books. 2016.)

The founder of The Boston Beer Company and Sam Adams Brewery shares his business lessons and remarkable story in this book. The book inspired me to pursue my own passions and shared great examples of how creating a positive spirit at work can lead to success.

You Are a Badass and *You Are a Badass at Making Money*, Jen Sincero (Sincero, Jen. *You Are a Badass.* Philadelphia, PA. Running Press Book Publishers. 2013 and Sincero, Jen. *You Are a Badass at Making Money.* New York, NY. Penguin Random House LLC. 2017.)

Both of these books led me to write this publication. I've read each of them three times! While they don't focus specifically on bringing joy to the workplace, each of these occasionally raunchy books will motivate you like nothing else to get excited about what you do in life and do it well enough to make a lot of money! And when you have that great combination, you'll naturally be joyful and spread it to others.

Cube Chic, Kelley L. Moore (Moore, Kelley L. *Cube Chic.* San Francisco, CA. Chronicle Books. 2006.)

This book will show you how to transform your drab cubicle or office into something amazing that you and your coworkers can enjoy every day. You'll love her various themes and ideas. As I mentioned earlier, you don't have to take every one of her suggestions to transform your workspace. But she'll inspire you to make at least a few changes!

Notes

[1] Kristi Hedges, https://www.forbes.com/sites/work-in-progress/2014/01/20/8-common-causes-of-workplace-demotivation/#7ce072da42c6

[2] Ansuya Harjani, https://www.cnbc.com/2013/09/17/nearly-half-of-the-worlds-employees-unhappy-in-their-jobs-survey.html

[3] Lydia Saad, http://news.gallup.com/poll/175286/hour-workweek-actually-longer-seven-hours.aspx

[4] Christine M. Riordan, https://hbr.org/2013/07/we-all-need-friends-at-work

[5] Jules Schroeder, https://www.forbes.com/sites/julesschroeder/2017/03/06/millennials-heres-why-youre-dissatisfied-at-work/#171762282846

[6] Shawn Achor, https://hbr.org/2012/01/positive-intelligence

[7] Gordon Tredgold, https://www.entrepreneur.com/article/281289

[8] Michael Ayers and Grover Porter, https://psychcentral.com/lib/what-is-emotional-intelligence-eq/

[9] Susan Adams, https://www.forbes.com/sites/susanadams/2015/06/18/money-doesnt-buy-happiness-at-work-new-study-says/#6c9fee9419bc

[10] Amy Morin, https://www.inc.com/amy-morin/science-says-your-bad-attitude-could-cost-you-3600-a-year.html

[11] Brianna Steinhilber, https://www.nbcnews.com/better/health/why-walking-most-underrated-form-exercise-ncna797271

[12] Anne Fisher, http://content.time.com/time/business/article/0,8599,1899915,00.html

[13] Emily Wyckoff, https://www.rachaelray.com/2012/05/17/ten-ways-to-jazz-up-water/

[14] Macaela Mackenzie, https://www.menshealth.com/nutrition/a19540772/healthy-snacking-before-sleep/

[15] Dana Sparks, https://newsnetwork.mayoclinic.org/discussion/tuesday-q-a-reducing-four-white-foods-in-your-healthy-diet-may-make-it-easier-to-eat-less-lose-weight/

[16] https://www.sleephealthfoundation.org.au/files/pdfs/Common-Causes-Inadequate-Sleep.pdf

[17] Ed Fraunheim and Sarah Lewis-Kulin, http://fortune.com/2016/04/26/giving-workers-paid-time-off-to-volunteer-will-help-your-company-succeed/

[18] Steve Dorfman, http://archive.constantcontact.com/fs075/1101536578069/archive/1101868203917.html

[19] Nicole Sforza, https://www.realsimple.com/home-organizing/decorating/what-feng-shui

[20] Kelley Moore, https://www.amazon.com/Cube-Chic-Kelly-Moore/dp/1594741050/ref=sr_1_1?ie=UTF8&qid=1522713210&sr=8-1&keywords=Cube+Chic

[21] Rachel Emma Silverman, https://www.wsj.com/articles/at-last-a-possible-solution-to-office-thermostat-wars-1489166854

[22] https://www.comfyapp.com/customers/appnexus/

[23] Nikki Tilley, https://www.gardeningknowhow.com/houseplants/hpgen/best-office-plants-good-plants-for-the-office-environment.htm

[24] http://www.alltrucking.com/faq/truck-drivers-in-the-usa/

[25] Ryan Whitwam, https://www.extremetech.com/computing/226867-comscore-computer-usage-falls-as-20-of-millennials-go-mobile-only

[26] Emily Conklin, https://www.entrepreneur.com/article/303551

[27] Gabrielle Dalvet, https://robinpowered.com/blog/office-loud-need-white-noise/

[28] Ray A. Smith, https://www.wsj.com/articles/why-dressing-for-success-leads-to-success-1456110340

[29] Jacquelyn Smith, https://www.forbes.com/sites/jacquelynsmith/2012/10/03/10-ways-to-get-your-colleagues-to-work-with-you-better/#4fe9f1004daf

[30] Jody Kohner, https://www.salesforce.com/blog/2017/02/what-is-salesforce-ohana.html

[31] Rob Desisto, https://www.salesforce.com/blog/2017/09/salesforces-ohana-culture-intern-experience.html

[32] Suzanne Lucas, https://www.inc.com/suzanne-lucas/why-employee-turnover-is-so-costly.html

[33] Emily Brandon, https://money.usnews.com/money/retirement/boomers/articles/2017-05-11/10-classic-and-unique-retirement-gift-ideas

[34] Lolly Daskal, President and CEO, Lead from Within, https://www.inc.com/lolly-daskal/how-to-deal-with-a-difficult-co-worker.html

Used by permission

[35] Shep Hyken, https://www.forbes.com/sites/shephyken/2017/05/27/how-happy-employees-make-happy-customers/#5c3021355c35

[36] Murray Goldstein, Cox Business, https://www.forbes.com/sites/coxbusiness/2015/10/20/the-importance-of-customer-service-in-driving-your-business/#505137791043

[37] Entrepreneur Staff, https://www.entrepreneur.com/article/226064

[38] Mariliza Karrera, https://www.careeraddict.com/benefits-networking

Used by permission

[39] Penny Brenden, http://www.theconnectingexperts.com/Blog/?category=2

Used by permission

[40] Elana Lyn Gross, https://www.forbes.com/sites/elanagross/2016/05/30/the-best-questions-to-ask-at-networking-events/#33b8acb9802a

www.ingramcontent.com/pod-product-compliance
Lightning Source LLC
Chambersburg PA
CBHW070046230426
43661CB00005B/783